DESIGN GUIDE
FOR STRUCTURAL HOLLOW SECTION
COLUMNS EXPOSED TO FIRE

OPOLITAN UNIVERSI

Learnir

12

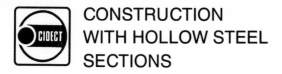

CONSTRUCTION
WITH HOLLOW STEEL
SECTIONS

Edited by: Comité International pour le Développement et l'Étude
de la Construction Tubulaire
Authors: Leen Twilt, TNO Institute for Building Materials and Structures, Delft
Rüdiger Hass, Hosser, Hass & Partner, Brunswick
Wolfram Klingsch, University of Wuppertal
Mike Edwards, Secretary CIDECT Stability and Fire Resistance Group
Dipak Dutta, Chairman of the Technical Commission of CIDECT

DESIGN GUIDE

FOR STRUCTURAL HOLLOW SECTION COLUMNS EXPOSED TO FIRE

L. Twilt, R. Hass, W. Klingsch, M. Edwards, D. Dutta

Verlag TÜV Rheinland

Die Deutsche Bibliothek – CIP Einheitsaufnahme

**Design guide for structural hollow section
columns exposed to fire** / [ed. by: Comité
International pour le Développement et l'Etude de
la Construction Tubulaire]. L. Twilt ... – Köln: Verl.
TÜV Rheinland, 1994
  (Construction with hollow steel sections)
  ISBN 3-8249-0171-4
NE: Twilt, Leen; Comité International pour le
  Développement et l'Étude de la Construction
  Tubulaire

ISBN 3-8249-0171-4

Preface

Steel in competition with concrete is often in a less favourable position, as a steel structure may lose its economy through additional fire protection requirements. The fire life of steel structures is therefore a problem that has to be faced from the onset of a project so that the most economical and best adopted solution may be found. Hollow sections offer a major advantage in this respect, as there is a large scope of improvement of fire protection by using them as regards cost and efficiency. For structures in hollow sections, it is possible to use protection methods other than externally interposing low thermal diffusion materials between the fire and the steel wall, for example, plaster, asbestos and vermiculite or paints and coatings designated as "intumescent" – methods specifically applicable to hollow sections namely filling the hollow space with concrete or water, static or circulating.

Besides the additional facilities for fire protection by concrete filling and water cooling, the hollow section also offers significant cost advantage over open sections, for example, I, L and U, through the reduced surface area to be protected.

All of the three fire protection methods, addition of materials on the external surface, concrete filling and water cooling have been described in this design guide showing the calculation procedures by means of diagrams and design examples.

Special emphasis has been given on the fire endurance behaviour of the concrete filled circular and rectangular hollow section columns, which has been one of the main fields of CIDECT research since late seventies. In the early eighties three extensive research programmes on this subject were carried out in France, Germany and the United Kingdom with the sponsorship of the European Community and the CIDECT. The tests were performed in the officially approved column furnaces of the following fire stations:

CSTB, Champs-sur-Marne (France)
CTICM, Maizières-les-Metz (France)
BAM, Berlin (Germany)
IBMB, Brunswick (Germany)
FIRTO, Boreham Wood (United Kingdom)

In 1986 the harmonization of all the test results were made by TNO, Delft in the framework of a CIDECT sponsored research. The fire resistance charts for composite hollow section columns evolving from this work has been incorporated into the ECCS (European Convention for Constructional Steelwork) recommendations as well as Eurocode 3 and 4.

This design guide is the fourth of a trilingual (English, French, German) series, which CIDECT is in the process of publishing during the recent years:

– Design guide for circular hollow section (CHS) joints under predominantly static loading
– Structural stability of hollow sections
– Design guide for rectangular hollow section (RHS) joints under predominantly static loading
– Design guide for structural hollow section columns exposed to fire
– Design guide for concrete filled hollow section columns
– Design guide for circular and rectangular hollow section joints under fatigue loading

The objective of this effort is to keep the architects, constructors and designers as well as the professors and the students of the technical universities and engineering schools up-to-date making them familiar with the latest developments and thereby enabling them to design with hollow sections appropriately.

Our sincere thanks go to the three well known experts in the field of fire engineering – Mr. Leen Twilt of TNO Delft, The Netherlands, Dr. Rüdiger Hass, Hosser, Hass & Partner, Brunswick and Professor Wolfram Klingsch, University of Wuppertal, Germany – who co-operated closely in writing this book. We specially thank Mr. Mike Edwards of British Steel Tubes & Pipes for his very valuable contributions.

Grateful acknowledgement is made to the CIDECT member firms for their support.

Dipak Dutta
Chairman of the Technical Commission
CIDECT

Contents

1   Introduction

Rectangular or circular hollow steel sections are often used in construction because of their structural efficiency and also because of their shape, when a visible architectural expression is required. The surface and profile of hollow steel sections are attractive and their high load bearing capacity leads to slim, economic and elegant constructions with large spans.

Unprotected structural hollow sections (SHS) have an inherent fire resistance of some 15 to 30 minutes. Traditionally, it has been assumed that unprotected steel members fail when they reach temperatures of about 450 to 550°C. However, the temperature at which a steel member reaches ultimate limit state, is dependent on the massivity of the section and the actual load level. If the load level of a column is less than 50% of the admissible load, the critical temperature rises to more than 650°C, which means for bare steel an increase in failure time of more than 20%.

When hollow steel sections are required to withstand extended periods in fire, additional measures, such as the following have to be taken to delay the rise in steel temperature:

– External insulation of the steel sections:

This type of fire protection can be applied to all kinds of structural elements (columns, beams and trusses). The temperature development in a protected hollow steel section depends on the thermal properties of the insulation material (conductivity), on the thickness of the insulation material and on the Shape Factor (massivity) of the steel profile.

External fire protection materials can be grouped as follows:
- insulating boards (based mainly on gypsum or mineral fibre or lightweight aggregates such as perlite and vermiculite);
- spray coating or plaster (based mainly on mineral fibre or lightweight aggregates such as perlite and vermiculite);
- intumescent coatings (paint-like mixtures, applied directly to the steel surface and swelling up in case of fire to a multiple of their original thickness);
- suspended ceilings (protecting mainly roofs, trusses);
- heat radiation shielding (thin steel panels used for external structures).

Intumescent coatings are restricted in some countries to a fire resistance of 30 or 60 min., but this technology is rapidly developing.

– Concrete filling of the section:

This type of fire protection is usually applied only to columns. To fill hollow sections with concrete is a very simple and attractive way of enhancing fire resistance. The temperature in the unprotected outer steel shell increases rapidly. However, as the steel shell gradually loses strength and stiffness, the load is transferred to the concrete core. Apart from the structural function, the hollow section also acts as a radiation shield to the concrete core. This leads, in combination with a steam layer between the steel and the concrete core, to a lower temperature rise in the core compared to reinforced concrete structures. Depending on the fire resistance requirements, the concrete in the hollow section can be plain concrete (fire resistance up to 60 min.) or concrete with rebars or steel fibres. New research aimed at increasing the fire resistance of concrete filled hollow sections is focused on the use of high strength concrete.

– Water cooling:

This type of fire protection can be applied to all kinds of hollow sections, but has been mostly used for columns. The hollow section acts at the same time as the load bearing structure and the water container. The protection system is quite sophisticated, needs a thorough design and proper hydraulic installations. The cooling effect consists of the absorption of heat by water, the removal of heat by water circulation and its consumption in the vaporization of water. In practical applications, these effects are combined. A suitably designed water filled system will limit the average steel temperature to less than 200°C. Two different systems can be used: permanently filled elements or elements filled only when a fire breaks out. In the latter case, protection depends on a fire detection system and a short water filling time. In unreplenished systems, the attainable fire resistance time is dependent on the total water content (including any reservoir tank) and on the shape of the heated structure. In systems where the water is constantly renewed, the fire resistance is unlimited.

Hollow sections can be used for all types of structural element, i. e. columns, beams, tension ties and lattice girder member. All can be made fire resistant. However, when using this manual, the following additional considerations also apply:

- the chapter on bare and protected steel can be applied to all SHS elements, but if board protection is to be used on members carrying tensile loads, care must be taken to ensure the integrity of joints between the boards;
- the use of unprotected concrete filled sections is restricted to columns;
- water cooling by natural flow is restricted to vertical or inclined elements in order to ensure the circulation of the water.

2 Fire resistance

2.1 Concept

Fire safety precautions are specified with the intent of avoiding any casualties and reducing economic fire damage to an acceptable level. For further background of required safety levels, see Chapter 2.2. As far as building construction is concerned, it is important that the construction elements can withstand a fire for a specified period of time. In this respect one should bear in mind that the strength and deformation properties of the commonly used building materials deteriorate significantly at the temperatures which may be expected under fire conditions. Moreover, the thermal expansion of most of the building materials appears to be considerable. As a result, the structural elements and assemblies may deform or even collapse, when exposed to fire conditions.

The time that a construction element can resist a fire depends largely on the anticipated temperature development of the fire itself. This temperature development is dependent, among other things, on the type and amount of combustible materials present[1] and on the fire ventilation conditions. Significant differences can be expected from case to case: see Fig. 2.1.

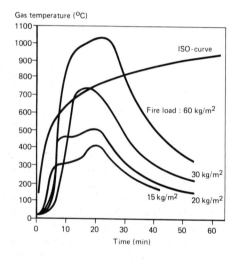

Fig. 2.1 – Natural fire curves

In practical fire safety design, however, it is the convention to use a time-temperature curve, which is more or less representative for post flash-over fires in buildings with relatively small compartments, such as apartment buildings and offices. This is the so-called "standard fire curve", defined in ISO 834 [1]. See Fig. 2.2. Alternative standard fire curves are in use in the USA [2] and for maritime applications [3]. Their differences from the ISO-curve are only small and of no practical significance.

The period of time during which a building component is able to withstand heat exposure according to the standard fire curve, is called the "fire resistance". In order to be able to determine the fire resistance of a building component, proper performance criteria have also to be determined. These criteria are defined in relation to the anticipated function of the respective building element during fire. In general, there are three such performance criteria:

---

[1] Usually, the amount of combustible materials is expressed in terms of kg wood per m² floor surface, called the fire load density.

- stability (R);
- insulation (I);
- integrity (E).

For details on the performance criteria, refer to, e.g. [1].

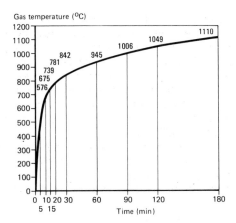

Fig. 2.2 – The standard fire curve

For building components such as columns, with only a load bearing function, the only relevant performance criterion is "stability". This is the criterion, therefore, which will be considered hereafter.

As far as the determination of the fire resistance is concerned, there are basically two possibilities: an experimental approach and an analytical or fire engineering approach.

The experimental approach, i.e. the determination of the fire resistance of columns on the basis of standard fire tests, is the traditional approach. Although based on different national testing procedures, the concept of fire testing is by and large the same in the various countries. Harmonization of the various national testing procedures, at least within the European Community, is on its way within CEN. See also Section 2.3, below.

The fire engineering approach is a relatively new development that has become possible due to the recent development of computer technology. In some but not all countries this approach has been accepted as an alternative to experimental assessment. On an international level, calculation rules for the fire resistance of both steel and composite steel concrete columns, including concrete filled SHS-columns, are under preparation, [4; 5][2].

As elucidated in Chapter 2.3 below, there are significant advantages to the analytical approach, when compared with the experimental one.

Important factors influencing the fire resistance of columns are:
- load level;
- shape and size of the cross section;
- buckling length.

Bare steel columns (i.e. SHS-columns without external protection or concrete filling) possess only a limited fire resistance. Depending on the load level and the Shape Factor (massivity), a fire resistance of 15 to 20 minutes is usually attainable; a 30 min. fire resistance can only be achieved in more exceptional cases. This situation may be dramatically improved by applying thermal insulation to the column. Depending on the type and thickness of the insulation material, fire resistances of many hours can be achieved, although most requirements today are limited to 120 minutes.

---

[2] This manual reflects the latest draft available at the time of writing.

SHS-columns filled with concrete have much higher load bearing capacity and longer fire resistance than unprotected empty SHS-columns. Provided the concrete is of good quality (over, say, C20) and the cross sectional dimensions are not too small (not less than 150 × 150 mm) a fire resistance of at least 30 minutes will be achieved. Sections with larger dimensions will have a higher fire resistance and by adding additional reinforcement to the concrete the fire resistance may be increased to over 120 minutes.

Infinite fire resistance can be achieved by water filling provided an adequate water supply is available.

Improved fire performance of SHS-columns can also be achieved by placing the columns outside the building envelope – an expedient often used for architectural purposes. By preventing direct flame impingement on the member, the need for additional fire protection measures can be significantly reduced or even become unnecessary.

It follows from the above discussion that the fire resistance of an SHS-column is not an inherent property of the column, but is influenced by a variety of design parameters. This is very important, since fire safety requirements for columns are normally expressed solely in terms of the fire resistance to be attained, and emphasizes the need to consider fire resistance requirements from the beginning in a structural design project. The background to these requirements and common levels for the required fire resistance are briefly discussed in the following section. For details of the design parameters and the design procedure, refer to chapters 3, 4 and 5 for empty, concrete filled and water filled SHS-columns respectively.

2.2 Requirements

Fire safety in buildings is concerned with achieving two fundamental objectives:
– to reduce the loss of life;
– to reduce the property or financial loss in or in the neighbourhood of a building fire.

In most countries the responsibility for achieving these objectives is divided between the government or civic authorities who have the responsibility for life safety via building regulations and the insurance companies who are concerned with property loss through their fire insurance policies.

The objectives of fire safety may be achieved in various ways. For example:
– by eliminating or protecting possible ignition sources, in order to prevent a fire occurring (fire prevention);
– by installing an automatic extinguishing device, in order to prevent the fire from growing into a severe fire (operational or active measures);
– by providing adequate fire resistance to the building components using passive or structural measures in order to prevent fire spreading from one fire compartment to adjacent compartments.

Often a combination of the above measures is applied. Ideally, the fire safety design concept should allow for a certain trade off between the various measures, i. e. emphasis on one or two of the possible measures should lead to relaxation of the remaining one(s). This would mean that the installation of, for example, a sprinkler system would lead to reduced overall requirements for the fire resistance. Such a trade off is not generally accepted at present but needs to be pursued with the appropriate authorities.

Requirements with regard to fire resistance clearly belong to the structural measures.

To date, the use of a conventional fire scenario based on the ISO standard fire curve is common practice in Europe and elsewhere. Safety levels in buildings relating to fully developed fire are mainly, but not exclusively, based on this approach and are verified against standard fire tests or a numeric simulation of them. The standard fire test is not intended to reflect the temperatures and stresses that would be experienced in real fires but provides a measure of the relative performance of elements of structures and materials within the capabilities and dimensions of the standard furnaces. In general, uncertainties about structural behaviour in real fires are taken into account by making conservative fire resistance requirements.

Required safety levels are specified in National Codes and normally depend on factors such as:
- type of occupancy;
- height and size of the building;
- effectiveness of fire brigade action;
- active measures such as vents and sprinklers (but not in all countries).

An overview of fire resistance requirements as a function of the number of storeys and representative for many European countries, is given in the following Table [6]:

Table 2.1 – Variations in required fire resistance

Type of building	Requirements	Fire class
One storey	None or low	Possibly up to R30
2 to 3 storey	None up to medium	Possibly up to R30
More than 3 storey	Medium	R60 to R120
Tall buildings	High	R90 and more

Although quite a large variation in requirements exists, one may conclude that in most countries the required fire resistance is not more than, say, 90 to 120 minutes. If such requirements are set, the minimum value is usually 30 minutes (some countries however have minimum requirements of 15 or 20 minutes). Intermediate values are usually given in steps of 30 minutes, leading to a scheme of 30, 60, 90, 120 minutes. The following general features may be identified:
- no specified fire resistance requirements for buildings with limited fire load density (say: 15–20 kg/m^2) or where the consequences of collapse of the structure are acceptable;
- fire resistance for a specified but limited period of time, where the time requirement is mainly intended to allow for safe evacuation of the occupants and intervention by rescue teams;
- extended fire resistance of the main structure to ensure that the structure can survive a full burn out of combustible materials in the buildings or a specified part of it.

It follows from the above discussion that unprotected steel may sometimes be sufficient. This holds for situations where fire safety is satisfied by other means (e. g. sprinklers) and/or if requirements with respect to fire resistance are only low (i. e. not beyond, say, 30 minutes).

When a fire resistance of 60 minutes or beyond is required, it is normally necessary to protect steel structures. At present, there is a variety of possibilities available to attain any required fire resistance level. Their application to SHS-columns is discussed in later chapters.

A full fire engineering approach, in which compartment and steel temperature are calculated from a consideration of the combustible material present, compartment geometry and ventilation, is becoming more accepted and has shown considerable savings in fire protection costs in specific cases.

2.3 Performance criteria

The fundamental concept behind all methods designed to predict structural stability in fire is that construction materials gradually lose strength and stiffness at elevated temperatures. For the different kinds of mild steel (cold worked or hot rolled) there is only a small difference in the reduction of material properties under high temperatures. In simple fire design, therefore there is often no need to differentiate between cold worked and hot rolled steel.

The reduction in the yield strength of structural steel and the compression strength of concrete with increasing temperature according to the Eurocodes is given in Fig. 2.3 [4; 5; 7].

Fig. 2.3 shows that there is not much difference in the relative reduction in strength of concrete and steel under high temperatures. The reason for the difference in the structural behaviour of steel and concrete elements under fire conditions is that heat propagates about 10 to 12 times

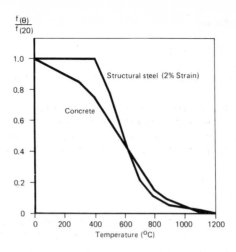

Fig. 2.3 – Schematic material strength reduction for structural steel and concrete according to [4; 5; 7]

faster in a steel structure than in a concrete structure of the same massivtiy, because the thermal conductivity of steel is higher than the thermal conductivity of concrete.

The fire resistance design of structures is normally based on similar static boundary conditions to the design under ambient temperature. In a multi-storey braced frame, the buckling length of each column at room temperature is usually assumed to be the column length between floors. However such structures are usually compartmented and any fire is likely to be limited to one storey. Therefore, any column affected by fire will lose its stiffness, while adjacent members will remain relatively cold. Accordingly, if the column is rigidly connected to the adjacent members, built-in end conditions can be assumed in the event of fire. Investigations have shown that in fire the buckling length of columns in braced frames is reduced to between 0.5 to 0.7 times the column length at room temperature, depending on the boundary conditions [8]. The more conservative effective length factor (0.7) should be used for assessing the buckling length in fire of columns on the top floor and for the columns at the edge of a building with only one adjacent beam. The higher reduction factor (0.5) may be used for all other columns. The schematic structural behaviour of columns in braced frames is shown in Fig. 2.4. The above rule is also applied in Eurocode 3 and 4, parts 1.2 [4; 5].

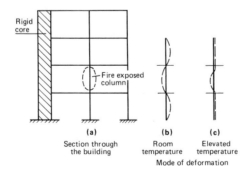

Fig. 2.4 – Schematic structural behaviour of columns in braced frames

The traditional method of demonstrating the performance of building elements in fire is the "standard fire resistance test". There are however many disadvantages related to fire testing, the most serious of which is the high costs involved. For economical and practical reasons it is not realistic to carry out fire tests for every combination of:

- steel section size and shape;
- cladding thickness;
- load level or stress distribution and
- column or beam length.

Another disadvantage of fire testing is the limitation in the field of application due to restrictions in specimen size.

Despite this, practical fire tests are still needed when special characteristics have to be assessed such as adhesion of the insulation to the structural member.

There is an increasing tendency to assess the fire resistance of individual members or sub-assemblies by analytical fire engineering. The Eurocodes on structural fire design define three levels of assessments:
- Level 1: Design Tables and Diagrams;
- Level 2: Simple Calculation;
- Level 3: General Calculation Procedures.

"General Calculation Procedures" is the most sophisticated level. Such calculation procedures include a complete thermal and mechanical analysis of the structure and use the values for the material properties given in the Eurocodes. General calculation methods enable real boundary conditions to be considered and take into account the influence of non-uniform temperature distribution over the section and therefore lead to more realistic failure times and consequently, to the most competitive design. However, the handling of the necessary computer programmes is quite time-consuming and requires expert knowledge. For practising engineers and architects not accustomed to handling specialised computer programs, "Simple Calculation Procedures" have been developed, which lead to a comprehensive design, but are limited in application range. They use conventional calculation procedures and provide normally adequate accuracy.

"Design Tables and Diagrams", which provide solutions on the safe side and allow fast design for restricted application ranges, form the lowest level of assessment.

In the following chapters, emphasis is given on the simple calculation procedures.

3 Designing unfilled SHS-columns for fire resistance

3.1 Basic principles

The calculation of the fire resistance of unfilled SHS-columns comprises of two steps:
- the determination of the temperature at which the column fails, the so called "critical steel temperature"; this is the mechanical response.
- the determination of the temperature development in the bare or protected steel section; this is the thermal response.

Both the above assume a uniform temperature distribution across the cross section and along the length of the steel member.

Combining the two calculation steps gives the time at which failure of the column would occur if exposed to standard fire conditions. This time is the fire resistance of the column. The calculation scheme is illustrated in Fig. 3.1.

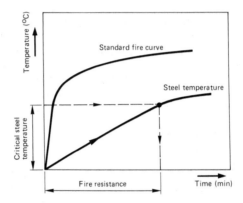

Fig. 3.1 – Calculation scheme for the fire resistance of steel elements

3.2 The mechanical response

The simple calculation rules for the critical temperature of steel columns discussed hereafter, hold for class 1, 2 and 3 cross-sections only (as defined in Eurocode 3, part 1-1 [10]) and can be applied both to protected and unprotected columns. For columns with a class 4 cross-section, a default value for the critical temperature of 350°C is be used.

The simple calculation rules for the critical steel temperature are commonly based on the axial load condition. In practical situations, however, a column will often be subjected to eccentric loading, see Fig. 3.2. In such cases, not only the axial force N but also the moment distribution (M_1, M_2) will play a role (see later).

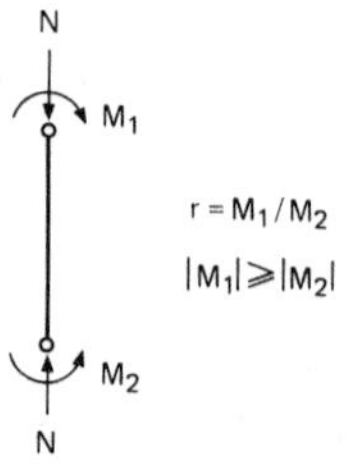

$$N$$

$$M_1$$

$$r = M_1 / M_2$$

$$|M_1| \geqslant |M_2|$$

$$M_2$$

$$N$$

Fig. 3.2 – Column under axial force and bending moments

16

The critical temperature of an axially loaded steel column depends on the ratio between the load which is present during a fire and the column minimum collapse load at room temperature. This ratio is called the degree of utilization (μ). For an axially loaded column:

$$\mu = N_{fi}/X_{min} \cdot R_{nc} \tag{1}$$

with:
N_{fi}: axial force in the fire situation,
R_{nc}: compression resistance of gross cross section at room temperature,
X_{min}: minimum buckling coefficient.

According to Eurocodes, see e. g. [4; 9], in the fire situation, generally only about 60% of the design load for normal conditions of use need to be taken into account. Also the partial safety factors, both for material properties and actions, are taken equal to unity.

The collapse load at room temperature is based on the given column dimensions in fire (see Section 2.3 above), but using the buckling curve "c" from Eurocode 3, Part 1.1 [10], irrespective of the type of SHS or its material.

The relation between the critical steel temperature and the modified degree of utilization ($c \cdot \mu$) is represented by Fig. 3.3, where c is an adaptation factor used to correct model simplifications. Eurocode 3, Part 1.2 [4] states that for columns under both axial and eccentric loading, c = 1.2. The modified degree of utilization ($c \cdot \mu$) can, in theory, vary between 1 and 0 and a high degree of utilization corresponds to a low critical temperature. (Theoretically, $c \cdot \mu = 1$ implies that the column is about to fail under room temperature conditions at a notional critical temperature of 20°C, while $c \cdot \mu = 0$ implies that there is no load on the column and the notional critical temperature will be as high as, say, 1200°C.)

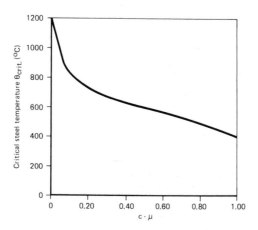

Fig. 3.3 – Critical steel temperature as a function of the modified degree of utilization ($c \cdot \mu$)

In the case of an eccentrically loaded column it is also possible to define an equivalent "degree of utilization". To do so, one must make use of an interaction curve which describes the critical combinations of normal force and applied moment. A commonly used interaction curve is:

$$\frac{N}{X_{min} \cdot R_{nc}} + \frac{k \cdot M}{R_{Mpl}} \leq 1 \tag{2}$$

with:
M: the maximum applied end-moment,
k: a reduction factor according to Eurocode 3, part 1.1,
R_{Mpl}: plastic moment of cross section at room temperature.

For the meaning of the other symbols, refer to Eq. (1).

17

The meaning of this formula is that any combination of moment and normal force which fulfils Eq. (2) can be resisted by the column (if the " = " sign hold, the column is about to fail). The degree of utilization for an eccentrically loaded column can now be defined as the value of the left hand side of Eq. (2) when the actual design values for the moment and the normal force are substituted into the equation. Hence:

$$\mu = \frac{N_{fi}}{X_{min} \cdot R_{nc}} + \frac{k \cdot M_{fi}}{R_{Mpl}} \tag{3}$$

Note that for an axial load, i. e. $M_{fi} = 0$, Eq. (3) reduces to Eq. (1).

The resulting value of μ must now be modified (using $c \cdot \mu$ as for an axially loaded column), after which the critical temperature can be read directly from Fig. 3.3.

The use of the degree of utilization in Eq. (3) above is, in effect, stating that the combined effect of a normal force and a moment on the critical temperature of an eccentrically loaded steel column is equal to that of an equivalent axial force (N_{eq}), provided both situations are characterized by the same degree of utilization (μ). The corresponding equivalent normal force (N_{eq}) follows from:

$$\frac{N_{fi}}{X_{min} \cdot R_{nc}} + \frac{k \cdot M_{fi}}{R_{Mpl}} = \mu = \frac{N_{eq}}{X_{min} \cdot R_{nc}} \tag{4}$$

so,

$$N_{eq} = N_{fi} + X_{min} \cdot R_{nc} \cdot \frac{k \cdot M_{fi}}{R_{Mpl}} \tag{5}$$

By means of the equivalent axial force, the critical temperature of an eccentrically loaded columns can easily be determined, using the simple calculation model, valid for axially loaded columns, see Fig. 3.3.

The above rule is used in Eurocode 3, part 1.2 [4]. Moreover, provided that a column has been designed to satisfy the room temperature requirements of Eurocode 4, Part 1 [4], a minimum default value of 510°C can be taken as the critical temperature of a steel column without any further analysis.

3.3   The thermal response

For unprotected steel sections, it can be shown that – for standard fire exposure – the temperature development of a steel section depends only on the relative geometry of the profile. This effect is taken into account by means of the Shape Faktor, A_m/V, where:

A_m = exposed surface area of the member per unit length [m^2/m];
V = volume of the member per unit length [m^3/m].

For a member unit length, this is identical to stating that:

A_m/V = exposed steel perimeter/steel cross section

The calculated curves presented in Fig. 3.4 illustrate the effect of the Shape Factor on the temperature development of an unprotected steel section when exposed to standard fire conditions.

For commonly used I-sections, Shape Factors are within a range of, say, 50 to 400 m^{-1}. For SHS profiles exposed to heat from all sides[3], the Shape Factor may be approximated by:

A_m/V = Perimeter/(Perimeter $\times$ thickness) = $1/t$

with: t = thickness of the steel hollow section.

---

[3] In the simple Eurocode calculation methods, based on actual observed performance in standard fire performance tests, a steel section is assumed to be equally exposed to fire on all four sides.

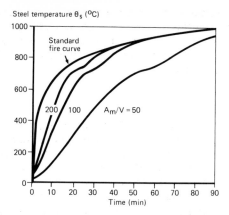

Fig. 3.4 – Calculated temperature development in an unprotected steel as a function of the Shape Factor

For a practical range of the SHS thickness of 20 to 2.5 mm, this also leads to Shape Factors varying between 50 and 400 m^{-1}.

For any given critical steel temperature, the fire resistance of an unprotected steel element – assuming standard fire conditions – depends only on its Shape Factor. This is illustrated in Fig. 3.5, where the time for unprotected steel members to reach a range of temperatures (450 – 600°C) is presented as a function of the Shape Factor. In many practical situations, the critical temperature of a steel member will be approximately 550°C, so the time to reach 550°C may be taken as a reasonable approximation of its fire resistance. This figure shows that an unprotected steel member with a Shape Factor smaller than approximately 40 m^{-1} may have a fire resistance of 30 minutes or beyond. The necessary Shape Factor to comply with any shorter fire resistance requirement can also be easily obtained from Fig. 3.5. In general, the fire resistance of an unprotected steel member is 30 minutes or less.

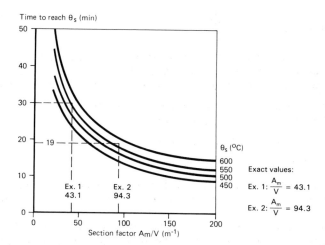

Fig. 3.5 – Time for an unprotected steel section to reach a given mean temperature under standard conditions as a function of the Shape Factor.

If external fire insulation is provided, the steel temperature development depends not only on the Shape Factor, but also on the type and thickness of the insulation material.

It is possible to construct charts which show how steel temperature varies with insulation thickness (d_i). Shape Factor (A_m/V) and time for a given insulation material, as illustrated in Fig. 3.6.

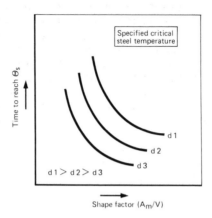

Fig. 3.6 – Fire resistance of insulated steel profiles as a function of the insulation thickness and the Shape Factor for a specified critical steel temperature.

3.4 Assessment method for fire insulation

The performance of a fire insulation system on structural steelwork depends on both the mechanical and the thermal behaviour of the system under fire conditions and is assessed on the basis of fire tests.

In these tests, both loaded and unloaded insulated steel profiles are exposed to standard fire conditions. The test specimens are selected to cover a practical application range of Shape Factors and insulation thicknesses. The larger loaded specimens (usually 3 – 5 m long) assess the ability of the insulation system to remain intact and adhere to the steel section (stickability). The tests on the smaller unloaded specimens (approximately 1 m long) evaluate and generalize the thermal characteristics of the insulation material. Compliance with a national assessment method is generally necessary to obtain access to that nation's market.

Although in most countries the concept of the assessment methods is similar, the details of the methods may differ quite significantly. Consequently, official test reports obtained in one country, are not always accepted in another country. With a view to change this situation, Eurocode 3, Part 1.2 [4] and the associated CEN standards will give harmonized rules. This work is currently being done and a first draft will be available for public comment in 1994.

3.5 Presentation of design information

For a given insulation material, the design of fire insulation for structural steelwork depends on only three parameters:
– required fire resistance;
– Shape Factor of the steel profile;
– thickness of the insulation material.

The fire resistance is the time at which a column 'fails', i.e. at which the steel temperature reaches the critical value. For the critical steel temperature, either default values can be taken (i.e. 510°C for columns according to Eurocode) or calculations can be undertaken. The latter option is given in many modern codes. In such an approach the critical steel temperature is defined as a function of the degree of utilization (see section 3.2).

The aim of the assessment methods for fire insulation of structural steel is to find a reliable relationship between the above three parameters. The presentation of the results differs from country to country. Fig. 3.7 gives some examples. In a design situation, when two of these parameters are known, the third one can be found from such graphs. Normally, the required fire resistance (i. e. the time to reach the critical steel temperature) will be the starting point. The necessary insulation thickness can then be found as a function of the Shape Factor and the critical steel temperature (or degree of utilization). By varying the design parameters in an appropriate way, an optimal design can be achieved. Interpolation between the curves given may be necessary. Fig. 3.8 exemplifies practical design graphs used in The Netherlands.

Modern assessment methods (e. g. the EC/CEN method mentioned above) allow not only a graphical presentation of the results, but also a presentation in terms of physical quantities (thermal conductivity, specific heat). This brings computer evaluation within reach. A variety of such computer programs is already available [11 ... 14]. Knowledge based computer programs are also under development, which offer the possibility of an easy, fast and reliable fire design without the need of having expert knowledge.

3.6 Construction details

Construction details significantly affect the stickability of the insulation system and therefore should be designed with care. Of special importance are:
– the condition of the steel surface when applying sprayed products;
– the design of joints, in the case of protective casings.
Any published fire safety assessment of an insulation system should give such details. These should include, for example, any special steel surface preparation, fixing systems, the type and distances of board connectors, the design of seals etc. and are normally specified in detailed drawings.

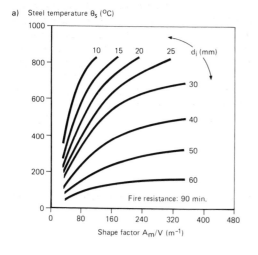
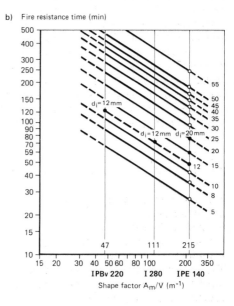

Fig. 3.7 – Ways of presenting the thermal characteristics of a typical fire insulation material in France (left) and Germany (right)

21

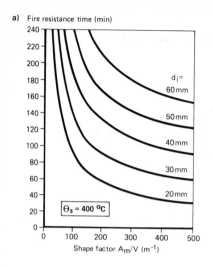

a) Fire resistance time (min)

Shape factor A_m/V (m^{-1})

$\Theta_s = 400\ ^oC$

$d_i = $
60 mm
50 mm
40 mm
30 mm
20 mm

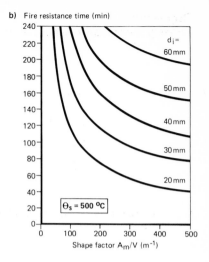

b) Fire resistance time (min)

Shape factor A_m/V (m^{-1})

$\Theta_s = 500\ ^oC$

$d_i = $
60 mm
50 mm
40 mm
30 mm
20 mm

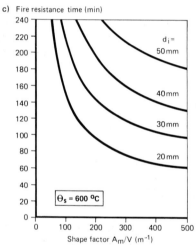

c) Fire resistance time (min)

Shape factor A_m/V (m^{-1})

$\Theta_s = 600\ ^oC$

$d_i = $
50 mm
40 mm
30 mm
20 mm

Fig. 3.8 – Fire resistance of insulated steel profiles as a function of the insulation thickness and the Shape Factor at critical temperatures of 400, 500 and 600°C (The Netherlands)

3.7 Design Examples

In this section the use of the design charts for protected and unprotected steel will be illustrated by means of three calculation examples using SHS sections to ISO/XIV-1982.

Example 1:

Assumptions:
An axially loaded, empty continuous SHS-column on an intermediate floor in a braced building as shown in Fig. 3.9:
– loading: 3,000 kN
– SHS section: hot rolled
– steel quality: Fe 360 (f_y = 235 N/mm²)

22

Requested:
To verify whether the column can be classified for R 30 fire resistance.

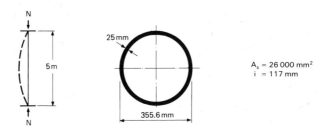

Fig. 3.9 – Axially loaded empty SHS-column ($\varnothing$ = 355.6 mm, t = 25 mm) on an intermediate floor of a braced building.

Solution:
The column is continuously connected with the columns above and below. Hence: buckling length: $L_{cr,\theta}$ = 0.5 × 5.00 = 2.50 m. Load bearing capacity under room temperature conditions is calculated according to EC3, part 1.1 [10], using the relative slenderness ratio $\overline{\lambda}_\theta$ for fire conditions:

$$\lambda_\theta = \frac{L_{cr,\theta}}{i} = \frac{2500}{117} = 21.4$$

and

$$\overline{\lambda}_\theta = \frac{1}{\pi}\frac{\lambda_\theta}{\sqrt{\dfrac{E_{20}}{\sigma_{e20}}}} = \frac{1}{\pi}\frac{21.4}{\sqrt{\dfrac{2.1 \cdot 10^5}{235}}} = 0.23$$

In fire design, the "c" buckling curve should be used, even for hot rolled SHS-sections. EC3, part 1 gives the following value for the buckling coefficient:

X_{min} = 0.99

Hence, the load bearing capacity under room temperature conditions is given by:

$X_{min} \cdot R_{nc}$ = 0.99 · 235 · 26,000 · 10^{-3} = 6,049 kN

With a correction factor of c = 1.2 for columns, the modified degree of utilization is given by:

$c \cdot \mu$ = 1.2 · 3,000/6,049 = 0.60

From Fig. 3.3: $\theta_{s,cr} \approx 560°C$

The Shape Factor is given by:

$A_m/V \approx 1/25 \cdot 10^{-3} \approx 40$ m^{-1}

From Fig. 3.5: the time to reach $\theta_{s,cr}$ = 560°C is about 30 minutes. Hence, the unprotected column can be classified having an intrinsic 30 minute fire resistance.
It should be noted that by room temperature design criteria, the column is over-dimensioned and uses a relatively heavy steel section.

Example 2:

Assumptions:
An axially loaded, empty continuous SHS-column on the top floor of a braced building, as shown in Fig. 3.10. An external protection is provided with thermal characteristics and available thicknesses given in Fig. 3.7a:
- loading: 2000 kN
- SHS section: hot rolled
- steel quality: Fe 510 (f_y = 355 N/mm²)

Requested:
To assess the necessary insulation thickness for a fire resistance of 90 minutes.

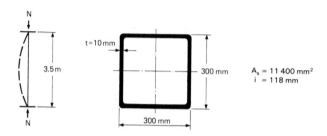

Fig. 3.10 – Axially loaded empty SHS-column ($\square$ = 300 mm, t = 10 mm) on an intermediate floor of a braced building.

Solution:
Since the column is on the top floor, there is no restraint from columns above. Hence: buckling length: $L_{cr,\theta}$ = 0.7 × 3.5 = 2.45 m. The load bearing capacity according to EC 3, part 1.1 [10] is calculated in a similar way as in the preceding example:

$$\lambda_\theta = \frac{2,450}{118} = 20.8$$

and

$$\bar{\lambda}_\theta = \frac{1}{\pi} \frac{20.8}{\sqrt{\dfrac{2.1 \cdot 10^5}{355}}} = 0.27$$

from which X_{min} = 0.97 for the hot rolled section (using buckling curve "c"); so the load bearing capacity for room temperature conditions is given by:

$$X_{min} \cdot R_{nc} = 0.97 \cdot 355 \cdot 11,400 \cdot 10^{-3} = 3,926 \text{ kN}$$

For the modified degree of utilization:

$$c \cdot \mu = 1.2 \cdot 2,000/3,926 = 0.61$$

From Fig. 3.3: $\theta_{s,cr} \approx 550°C$

The Shape Factor is given by:

$$A_m/V \approx 1/10 \cdot 10^3 \approx 100 \text{ m}^{-1}$$

It follows from Fig. 3.7a that a thickness of 20 mm external fire protection is necessary.
Note that, according to Fig. 3.5 the fire resistance for the unprotected SHS is only 19 minutes. This is due to the relatively high Shape Factor.

Example 3:

Assumptions:
An eccentrically loaded, empty continuous SHS-column on an intermediate floor in a braced building as shown in Fig. 3.11:
– normal force: 1000 kN
– end moments: 75 kNm
– SHS section: hot rolled
– steel quality: Fe 510 (f_y = 355 N/mm²)
External protection material of 20 mm thickness with thermal properties according to Fig. 3.8 is applied.

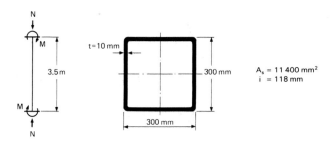

Fig. 3.11 – Eccentrically loaded empty SHS column ($\Box$ = 300 mm, t = 10 mm) on an intermediate floor of a braced building

Requested:
To verify whether the fire resistance of the column is 120 minutes.

Solution:
The column is continuously connected with the columns above and below. Hence: buckling length: $L_{cr,\theta}$ = 0.5 × 3.50 = 1.75 m. Cross sectional dimensions and steel quality of the column are the same as in example 2. Hence:

$$\overline{\lambda}_\theta = 0.27 \cdot 1750/2450 = 0.19$$

The equivalent normal force is calculated by applying eq. (5) of section 3.2 and follows with:

N_{fi} = 1,000 kN
X_{min} = 1 (see EC3, part 1.1)
R_{nc} = 355 · 11,400 · 10^{-3} = 4,047 kN
k   = 1 (see EC3, part 1.1)
M_{fi} = 75 kNm
R_{Mpl} = 355 · 1,238,000 · 10^{-6} = 439 kNm

So, from eqn. (5):

N_{eq} = 1,000 + 1 · 4,047 · 1 · 75/439 = 1,691 kN

Hence, the modified degree of utilization is:

$c \cdot \mu$ = 1.2 · 1,691/4,047 = 0.50

From Fig. 3.3: $\theta_{s,cr} \approx$ 600°C

The Shape Factor is as in example 2: $A_m/V \approx$ 100 m⁻¹.

It follows from Fig. 3.8c that for a fire protection thickness of 20 mm and a critical steel temperature of 600°C a fire resistance of 140 minutes is obtained. Since this time exceeds 120 min, the column may be classified as R 120.

4 Designing concrete filled SHS-columns for fire resistance

4.1 Basic principles

In a fire, the resulting temperature distribution in an empty SHS-column, whether unprotected or externally protected, is more or less uniform. In contrast, the heating behaviour of a concrete filled SHS-column is significantly different: combining materials with markedly different thermal conductivities produces extreme transient heating behaviour and high temperature differentials across the cross-section.

It is because of these differentials that concrete filled SHS-columns can be designed to have a fire resistance of up to 120 minutes or more without external protection. However, simple calculation models for fire design based on the Shape Factor (massivity) A_m/V cannot be used. Instead, a special fire design method is necessary, that takes into account the different thermal characteristics of the various materials and the resulting transient heating [15].

4.2 Unprotected columns – thermal and mechanical response

Because of their different location in the cross section, the various components of a concrete filled SHS-column will each have different time dependent strength reduction characteristics.

The unprotected, directly exposed steel shell will be rapidly heated and will show a significant strength reduction within a short time.

The concrete core with its high massivity and low thermal conductivity will, for a time, maintain a significantly high proportion of its strength, mostly in the core area rather than near the surface.

Reinforcement, if used, is normally placed near the surface but is protected by, typically 25 – 50 mm of concrete. For this reason, there will be a retarded strength reduction.

Figure 4.1 demonstrates this characteristic behaviour and may be considered as the basic diagram for describing the fire performance of concrete filled SHS-columns.

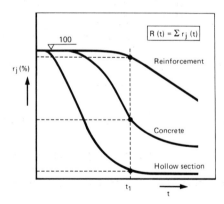

Fig. 4.1 – Typical strength reduction characteristics of the various components of a concrete filled SHS-column.

The load bearing capacity R of a cross section is the sum of the load bearing capacities of each of its components r_j. In the fire case, all component capacities are dependent on the fire endurance time t.

$$R(t) = \Sigma\, r_j\, (t)$$

In room temperature design the steel shell is likely to be the dominant load bearing component because of the high strength of the steel and the location of the profile. However, after a fire time t_1, only a small percentage of the original load bearing capacity of the steel shell can still be activated. This means that in the fire case the main part of the load carried by the steel section will be redistributed to the concrete core, which loses strength and stiffness more slowly than the steel section. If this re-distributed load were to overstress the concrete, the column would fail within a short time. The following may, therefore, be concluded:
– the load bearing capacity of the steel shell should be minimized which means thin shell thickness and low steel grade;
– the load bearing capacity of the concrete core should be optimised, which means higher concrete strength and reinforcement.

The above also means that differences in hollow section characteristics – such as whether it is seamless, welded, hot finished or cold formed – will not significantly influence the fire behaviour of a concrete filled SHS-column.

With room temperature design it is easy to obtain a high load bearing capacity for rather small cross sectional dimensions. But with small cross sectional dimensions the fire resistance is normally limited. Fig. 4.2 shows a comparison of the heating behaviour of two circular SHS sections of different diameters. From this figure, it is obvious that the smaller section will be heated up so rapidly that a significant fire resistance time will only be reached at a low level of applied load.

Since the strength reduction of the components is directly affected by the relative heating characteristic of the cross section, a minium column cross sectional dimension is often necessary to fulfil a required fire resistance.

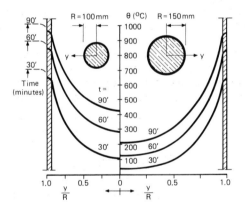

Fig. 4.2 – Relative heating of different sized concrete filled SHS columns

With increasing temperature, strength and Young's modulus decrease. Thus, load bearing capacity of a structural member decreases with time while its deformation increases. In practical fire design, the influence of the column slenderness also has to be taken into account.

Fig. 4.3 demonstrates the time dependent decrease of the overall resistance R_1 of a composite structural member [14]. When member resistance R_1 has dropped to the level of the acting loading S_1, the failure time $t_{fr(1/1)}$ has been reached.

Fig. 4.3 also demonstrates the different basic possibilities to influence the failure time t_{fr} (= fire resistance time).

At a lower load level S_2, the intersection point with the column load bearing characteristic R_1 will be shifted from $t_{fr(1/1)}$ to $t_{fr(2/1)}$. This is equivalent to increasing fire resistance by over-design, which is a rather conservative but, sometimes, effective method. A better method to reach a higher failure time t_{fr} is to improve the resistance of the structural member itself: shifting the curve from R_1 to R_2 by member fire design. The failure time will increase from $t_{fr(1/1)}$ to $t_{fr(1/2)}$.

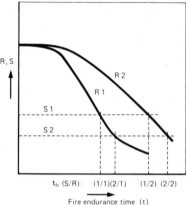

Fig. 4.3 – Load bearing capacity of concrete filled SHS-columns as a function of time.

Both above methods can be combined; improved member design (R_2) and lower utilization (S_2) will lead to failure point t_{fr} (2/2).
These philosophies underpin the design methods discussed below.

4.3 Assessment methods for unprotected columns

4.3.1 Levels of assessment

Design rules for concrete filled SHS-columns are presented in Eurocode 4, Part 1.2 [5]. As already explained in Chapter 2.3, in the Eurocodes, assessment on three different levels is foreseen:
– Level 1: Tabulated data;
– Level 2: Simple calculation models;
– Level 3: General calculation models.
This design guide deals with design information on level 1 and 2, i.e. tabulated data and simple calculation models, including the respective application ranges. For more general calculation models, refer to [10; 11; 13].

4.3.2 Level 1 design: tabulated data

Using Table 4.1, unprotected concrete filled hollow section columns may be classified according to:
– the degree of utilization (μ)
– the minimum cross section size (b or d),
– the amount of reinforcement (%) ($p_r = [A_r/(A_c + A_r)] \cdot 100$)
– the minimum axis distance of the reinforcement bars (d_r).
The degree of utilization μ is given by: (see also section 3.2)

$$\mu = N_{fi}/R_d$$

with:
N_{fi} = axial force in the fire situation,
R_d = the design resistance at room temperatrure

and is calculated according to the room temperature procedures of EC4, Part 1 [16]. However, the following additional limitations apply:

Table 4.1 – Minimum cross-sectional dimensions, reinforcement ratios and axis distances of the re-bars for fire resistance classification for various degrees of utilization μ

Steel section b/t > 25 or d/t > 25	Fire Resistance Class				
	R30	R60	R90	R120	R180
Minimum cross-sectional dimensions for $\mu = 0.3$					
Minimum width (b) or diameter (d)	160	200	220	260	400
Minimum % of reinforcement (p_r)	0	1.5	3.0	6.0	6.0
Minimum depth of re-bar centre (d_r)	–	30	40	50	60
Minimum cross-sectional dimensions for $\mu = 0.5$					
Minimum width (b) or diameter (d)	260	260	400	450	500
Minimum % of reinforcement (p_r)	0.0	3.0	6.0	6.0	6.0
Minimum depth of re-bar centre (d_r)	–	30	40	50	60
Minimum cross sectional dimensions for $\mu = 0.7$					
Minimum width (b) or diameter (d)	260	450	500	–	–
Minimum % of reinforcement (p_r)	3.0	6.0	6.0	–	–
Minimum depth of re-bar centre (d_r)	25	30	40	–	–

- Irrespective of the actual steel grade, the yield strength of the SHS is limited to a maximum of 235 N/mm²;
- The wall thickness of the steel is limited to a maximum of 1/25 of the main cross sectional dimension;
- Reinforcement ratios higher than 3% are not taken into account.

4.3.3 Level 2: calculated model

A level 2 computer program has been developed and verified by Valexy, the French member of CIDECT, to model the fire performance of concrete filled SHS-columns [17]. This program has been modified in order to reach compliance with more recent test results [18]. In its present version, it forms the basis of the Eurocode buckling curves for concrete filled SHS-columns at elevated temperatures: design charts have been developed in which, for a standard fire exposure of (30), 60, 90 and 120 minutes, the collapse load $N_{cr,\theta}$ of concrete filled SHS-columns is given as a function of the buckling length $L_{cr,\theta}$. A typical chart is illustrated in Fig. 4.4. For any combination of applied load and buckling length the relevant fire resistance class can easily be determined. The combination indicated in Fig. 4.4, for example, leads to a fire resistance rating of 60 minutes.

It is assumed that the loading will remain constant during the fire process, i. e. restraint forces do not play a role. These conditions normally apply during standard fire resistance tests as well. Moreover, the design charts are for axial loading only. Refer to Section 3.3 for a conceptual method, also applicable to composite columns in fire, by which the effect of eccentric loading on the fire resistance can be taken into account.

The value for buckling length depends on the boundary conditions, as described in Section 2.2.

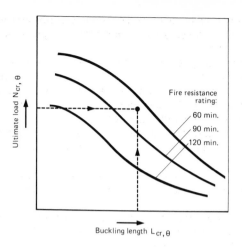

Fig. 4.4 – Buckling curves for different fire resistance classes (qualitative)

For a given buckling length and loading, the fire resistance of concrete filled SHS-columns depends mainly on the cross sectional dimensions, the concrete quality and the reinforcement, if any. By a proper choice of these parameters, practically any fire resistance can be met. If no reinforcement is used and the column is under its maximum design load at room temperature conditions, a fire resistance of 30 minutes can normally be achieved; 60 minutes is however not attainable unless the load level is significantly decreased. This is why the design charts focus on fire resistances of 60 minutes and more and only reinforced SHS-columns are taken into account.

In Annex I a full set of design graphs is presented [5; 19]. For a review of the various options, refer to Table I.1 of this Annex.

When calculating the design charts, the largest of the following values has been taken for the concrete cover d_r, as shown in Fig. 4.5:

d_r = 30 mm
d_r = b/8 or d/8 mm

with:
b, d = side length or diameter of the SHS section.

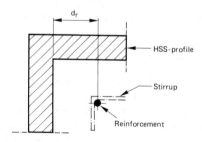

Fig. 4.5 – Concrete cover d_r

4.4 Unprotected columns – technological aspects

Normally SHS composite columns will comprise of the following components:
– the hollow section;
– concrete with or without reinforcement.

Just filling a hollow section with concrete or mortar will not activate the advantages of composite construction. It is necessary to combine all the components in such a way that they continue to act together in fire.

Concrete quality should be designed to fulfil the required load bearing capacity of the core under fire conditions. In general, there are no special requirements for the type of cement or aggregates. Maximum size of the coarse aggregate should take into account the geometrical situation of the hollow section (e. g. the SHS profile's internal dimension, the distance between the stirrups and the SHS profile's internal surface).

The concrete filling of the column must be done with care. Good concreting practice should be maintained in order to ensure sufficient fire performance. Internal or external vibrators should, therefore, be used.

The location of the reinforcing bars must be fixed by the use of stirrups and spacers. Stirrups need not be designed for shear forces because of the high shear force resistance of the hollow section in the fire case.

Concrete filling can be done either prior to assembly or after erection of the structure. Normally, preconcreting will be chosen only for single storey columns because of the weight limitations of a completely filled column. For multi-storey continuous columns, a complete erection of the structure without concrete is both possible and normally preferable. In that case, the concrete should be pumped into the hollow sections from the bottom, to guarantee a complete filling of the multi-storey continuous columns. Care in joint detailing is needed to ensure free flow of the concrete.

Small drain holes (10 to 15 mm dia.) are required in the walls of the SHS, usually in pairs. Such holes must be provided for each storey length at each floor level, with a maximum distance of 5.0 m between pairs. They must be placed between 100 and 120 mm from each column end. Those holes are intended to prevent the bursting of the column under steam pressure from the heating of entrapped water in the enclosed concrete.

Beside the standard SHS cross sections, a variety of different cross section designs have also been developed in the past and successfully used for building projects. They are all based either on combinations of hollow sections (tube inside tube) or on combinations of hollow sections with other steel profiles. The advantages of such special cross section types are an increased load bearing capacity without the need to increase the outer cross sectional dimensions, or reduced dimensions for a given load capacity.

To fulfil architectural requirements, special steels, such as weathering steel, can also be used for the SHS of the columns.

Careful design of the top and bottom of a single column or at the joints of a continuous column is necessary to ensure that the loading is introduced into the composite cross section in a proper way. Advice on the good fire design of joints is given in Chapter 6.

4.5 Externally protected concrete filled SHS-columns

If an extended fire resistance is desired, in combination with a high load level and/or a minimised column cross-section, it may be necessary to apply conventional external protection to a concrete filled SHS-column. If the thickness of the protection material is such, that the temperature of the steel section does not exceed 350°C[4], it may be assumed that the criterion R ("stability") for the column is met [5]. A CEN test method, based on this assumption for determining the necessary protection thickness is under preparation [20]. In this method, test specimens are selected such that both the cohesive and insulative properties of the fire protection insulation material are assessed. For this reason, at least one loaded full size SHS-column with minimum thickness of the applied insulation system should be tested. Additionally, unloaded small size specimens may be tested. Results are presented in a graphical plot. For an illustration, see Fig. 4.6. Linear interpolation is allowed, provided that

---

[4] This temperature reflects the present provisional state of the draft CEN-standard.

the test results refer to test specimens with SHS cross sections with identical geometry and physical properties. Extrapolation rules are given in [18] as well. The most important ones are that the assessment results may be used also in situations where:
– the thickness of the steel wall is greater than tested;
– all dimensions of the cross section are greater than tested;
– the concrete density is greater than tested.

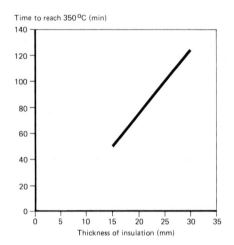

Fig. 4.6 – Presentation of the assessment results for an external fire protection for SHS-columns (qualitative).

As an alternative to the above more or less conventional approach, one may undertake an analytical interpretation of the test results. So far however, no generally accepted calculation models and/or design charts are available.

4.6 Design examples

In this section the use of the design charts given in Annex I, will be illustrated by means of two calculation examples.

Example 1:

Assumptions:
An axially loaded, continuous SHS-column on top floor:
– loading: 280 kN
– column length: 5.00 m
– SHS section: 220 × 220 × 6.3 mm
– steel quality: Fe 360
– concrete quality: C 40
– reinforcement quality: S 400
– percentage of reinforcement: p_r = 2.5%

Requested:
Check whether the column can be classified for 90 minutes fire resistance.

Solution:
The column is situated on top floor and continuously connected to the column below; hence, buckling length: 0.7 × 5.00 = 3.50 m.

Relevant design chart: I 27
Relevant curve: 8

From the relevant curves for a buckling length of 3.50 m and the given column geometry and material qualities, the collapse load after 90 minutes standard fire exposure is 316 kN; actual loading is 280 kN, hence the column is classified for 90 minutes fire resistance.

Example 2:

Assumptions:
An axially loaded, continuous SHS-column at an intermediate floor of a high rise building:
– loading: 1330 kN
– column length: 3.00 m.

Requested:
The available alternative column design to give a fire resistance rating of 60 minutes with a width (diameter) less than 280 mm.

Solution:
The column is continuously connected with the columns above and below; hence, buckling length: $0.5 \times 3.0 = 1.5$ m.

Relevant design diagrams: I 7, I 28 and I 31.
Diagram I 7:   circular SHS-section $\varnothing$ 273 $\times$ 5 mm;
                 curves 6 to 8
                 e. g.: curve 8: concrete grade: C40
                                  reinforcement: $p_r = 2.5\%$.
Diagram I 28: square SHS-section $\square$ 250 $\times$ 6.3 mm;
                 curves 6 to 9
                 e. g.: curve 6: concrete grade: C30
                                  reinforcement: $p_r = 4.0\%$.
Diagram I 31: square SHS-section $\square$ 260 $\times$ 6.3 mm;
                 curves 5 to 9
                 e. g.: curve 7: concrete grade: C40
                 reinforcement: $p_r = 1.0\%$.

5 Designing water filled SHS-columns for fire resistance

5.1 Basic principles

There are several ways to implement the principle of water cooling of SHS-columns. However, only water cooling by permanent water filling will be discussed in this design guide. Non-permanent filling, pumped flow systems and external water cooling of the steel with sprinklers or similar equipment are outside the scope of this manual, because they are active methods, not structural methods using natural circulation.

Water filling using natural circulation provides a safe and reliable fire protection method for SHS-columns, if two conditions are satisfied [21; 22]:
– the system is self activating in fire;
– the system is self controlling.

In a properly designed system, the natural circulation will be activated when the columns are locally heated by the outbreak of a fire. The density of warm water is lower than the density of cold water, which produces the pressure differentials that activate the natural circulation. The effect will be intensified when localised boiling commences and steam is formed, since the mixture of water and steam bubbles has a significantly lower density than hot water. As the fire develops further, the rate of steam production will also increase, thus forcing the cooling effect obtained by naturally activated circulation. This behaviour can be seen as a self controlling effect, since the cooling effect itself will be intensified as the fire severity increases.

The following methods of permanent water filling are available:

Unreplenished columns (UC)

Simply filling a column with water, with no provision for replacing any water lost through steam production, will lead to an increased, but limited fire resistance compared to that of the empty column. In multi-storey columns, the fire resistance may be increased by externally protecting the top storey length and using it as a reservoir for the lower stories. However, heavy steam production may lead to an additional critical loss of water by steam bubble eruption. This column type should be used only for lower fire resistance requirements, not beyond, say, 60 minutes. Its economical advantage is limited.

Columns with external pipe (CEP)

This system has a connecting down pipe between the bottom and top of the columns. The lighter, upwards flowing water-steam mixture must be separated at the top, so that the water can return down through the pipe to the bottom. In this manner an external naturally forced circulation will be activated. In addition, the pipe can be connected with a water storage tank at the top of the building to replace the water lost from steam production and possibly act as a common water/steam separating chamber. A group of individual columns can be connected at their bottom to a shared connecting pipe as well as with a connecting pipe at the top. For such a group of columns, only one down pipe is necessary, connecting top and bottom of the whole group. Fig. 5.1 a shows the principle of CEP columns.

Columns with internal pipe (CIP)

In this system, an internal down tube is used within each column to provide a supply of cool water to the bottom of each column. This promotes the internal, naturally activated circulation of the upward flowing water-steam mixture and the down flowing water after steam separation. Thus, each column acts as an individual member without any connection to the other columns.

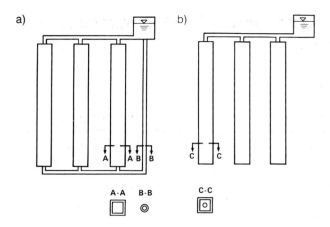

Fig. 5.1 – Options for columns with external and internal pipes (CEP versus CIP)

To minimize the number of water storage tanks, the tops of several CIP columns can be connected by a common pipe leading to one storage tank for the whole group. Fig. 5.1 b shows the principle of CIP columns.

Mixed systems

CEP and CIP columns can be mixed within a building and they can be connected to act as a mixed integrated system. This can be advantageous for structures containing not only columns, but also water filled diagonals for bracing etc.
In the naturally circulating systems described above, water filling cannot be used with horizontal members for physical reasons. A safe design needs a minimum declination of about 45°.
It is not advising to use any electro-mechanical installation such as pumps, actuated valves and the like. There is a danger of the pumps acting against the naturally produced circulation. This may lead to a failure of the cooling system and thus, to a collapse of the water filled structure.

5.2 Assessment methods

A careful design is necessary to ensure the positive behaviour of a water filled SHS-column system. Different fire scenarios may have to be checked to decide a worst case situation for the system design. Two main criteria must be fulfilled to ensure the cooling effect:
– natural circulation of the water is maintained;
– water losses due to steam production are replaced.
The mass of the water cooled steel structure as well as the water within the system can be taken into account when calculating the time of the commencement of boiling. The loss of water mass by evaporation has only to be estimated for the time difference between the start of boiling and the required fire resistance time.
For the characteristic thermal behaviour, refer to Fig. 5.2.
The maximum temperature reached by the steel can be estimated from the boiling temperature of the water filling. The boiling temperature itself depends on the hydraulic water pressure, i. e. the static head. In addition, there will be a temperature gradient across the wall of the hollow section, which will lead to a slight increase of the temperature of the steel surface directly exposed to the fire. However, the maximum external steel surface temperature will normally not reach a value high enough to significantly affect the mechanical properties of the

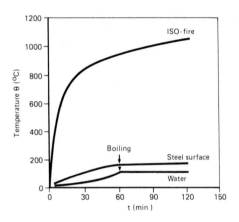

Fig. 5.2 – Typical temperature development in a water filled SHS-column, exposed to standard fire conditions

steel. Apart from situations in which extreme high values of shell thickness and water pressure apply (e. g. columns in high-rise buildings), the load bearing capacity and stiffness of a water filled SHS-column can be assumed as independent of any fire attack, as long as the natural circulation of the cooling system continues.

Usually it will be necessary to develop or use a computer program to quantify this procedure. The following assumptions are typical of those that would be made:

I.   The columns are exposed to the standard ISO fire.
II. The cumulative heat flow regime can be represented by a quasi steady state summation based on ONE minute time intervals using the average of the furnace temperature over each time interval.
III. Heat transfer coefficients between the fire and the external surface of the SHS conform to EC1 [9] Part 10.

i. e., $Q = 25 \cdot (T_f - T_s) + 2.81232 \cdot 10^{-8} \cdot ((T_f + 273)^4 - (T_s + 273)^4)$ W/m²

where: T_f = temperature of the fire
T_s = temperature at the outer surface of the SHS

IV. Conduction through the column wall obeys a simple Fourier relationship.

$Q = k_s/x_s \cdot (T_s - T_i)$ W/m²

where: $k_s = (54 - 0.0333 \cdot T_s)$ W/m°C
and x_s = SHS wall thickness
T_i = temperature at the inner surface of the SHS

V.   There is a bubble layer at the steel/water interface layer. Heat flow through obeys a simple power law.

$Q = A \cdot 1000 \cdot (T_i - T_w)^B$ W/m²

where: T_w = boiling temperature of the water

for water: $A = 2.2411 : B = 1.6322$

Comment: – Equation was developed to describe the graph in Fig. 5.3 [22], which predicts $(T_i - T_w)$ for heat flux densities up to 250 kW/m²

VI. The cooling water absorbs heat by local heating from 20°C to 100°C and is then vaporised.

so,   h (total) = 4.187 · 80 + 2150 = 335 + 2150 = 2485 kJ/kg

36

where, h (total) is the heat absorption per unit mass.

VII. The boiling temperature of water under pressure (T_w) also obeys a simple power law.

$$T_w = 53.853 \cdot (P + 10.33)^{.264} \quad \text{(but } T_w \text{ not less than 100°C)}$$

where P is the pressure head in metres of H_2O

Comment: – Equation was developed to describe the graph in Fig. 5.4 [22] which predicts T_w for pressure heads up to 60 m.

The Tables 5.1 and 5.2 are derived from such a computer program and are based on the theory explained in [22], but with the heat transfer coefficients between the fire and the external surface of the SHS conforming to those given in Eurocode 1, part 2.7 [9] and Eurocode 3, part 1.2 [4].

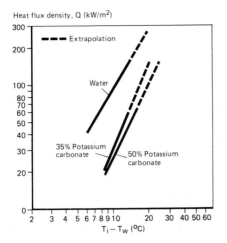

Fig. 5.3 – Temperature drop, steel to circulatory fluid

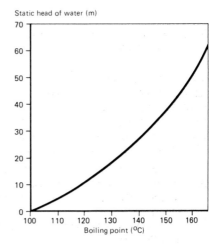

Fig. 5.4 – Boiling point of water under pressure

Table 5.1 shows temperatures assessed using these assumptions, based on the ISO "standard fire" in a single storey building or the top storey of a building where the water is at atmospheric pressure. The water in any lower storey column will be under pressure and will boil at temperatures higher than 100°C. Consequently, such columns will attain slightly higher temperatures during a fire and so will need slightly less water for protection.

Table 5.1 – Estimated external SHS wall temperatures

SHS wall thickness	Fire Time (minutes)			
	30	60	90	120
(mm)	SHS external temp. (°C)			
5	114	117	120	122
10	120	125	129	132
15	126	134	139	143
20	132	145	149	155
25	138	150	159	166

Most Structural Hollow Sections have walls with less than 25 mm thickness. An estimated water pressure head of at least 24 m will be needed to raise the external temperature of a

25 mm thick SHS to 200°C. Similarly, an estimated pressure head of at least 80 m will be needed to raise the external temperature of a 25 mm thick RHS to 250°C. Consequently, in practical situations, the steel temperature is well below its critical value. See also 3.2.

Table 5.2 below is a simple design table giving the estimated water requirements under ISO "standard fire" heating, again based on the worst case of a fire in the top storey of a building. This table is intended to enable a design engineer to make a preliminary estimate of the weight of water required for a desired fire life, the resulting tankage and hence the additional dead loads to impose on the structure. It is assumed that there is no circulation of the water prior to boiling and no bulk heating occurs, i. e. the thermal capacity of the rest of the system in a local fire is ignored.

Table 5.2 – Estimated total water requirement per m² heated column surface

Fire Time (minutes)	30	60	90	120
Water required (kg/m²)	30	82	147	222

In any full design procedure, the pressure head losses generated by the required circulation of steam and water in the respective piping systems would then be calculated and a check made that the system would perform properly when they were imposed.

5.3 Technological aspects and constructional details

The cooling medium denoted in this chapter as "water" is, in fact, a mixture of water with anti-corrosion and anti-freezing additives.

Potassium Nitrate can be used as an anti-corrosion additive at a typical concentration of 1 kg KNO_2/m^3 water.

Potassium Carbonate (K_2CO_3) is normally used as an anti-freezing additive. Its concentration depends on the lowest (sub-zero) temperature for which the cooling system has to be designed. The amount of this additive cannot be neglected since it will influence both the physical and thermodynamic behaviour of the liquid: the resulting higher liquid density must be taken into account in the static pressure calculations, so that the boiling temperature will depend on its concentration. Its presence may also alter the heat transfer characteristics of the bubble layer at the internal steel/water interface layer. In addition, the concentration of the K_2CO_3 in the liquid may increase as the volume of water is reduced by evaporation. Accordingly, after a severe fire an inspection of the pipework system has to be made to check that no carbonate has solidified in them.

To guarantee that the cooling system performs safely in fire, a number of details have to be assessed or designed very carefully, such as:
- the method to be used to separate the upward flowing water-steam mixture and the downward flowing water,
- the location and dimension of the steam outlet pipe,
- the steam reservoir, if any, in the water storage tank,
- the minimum water level in any storage tank at the end of the required fire resistance time,
- the relationship between internal pipe and column sizes for CIP-system or between external connecting pipes and column for CEP-system,
- the hydrodynamic performance of both the water and steam piping systems, including joints, bends, orifices, etc.,
- the fire protection of the water storage tank and any external pipes,
- the pressure safety of the whole system, depending on both the static head and the additional steam pressure,
- the quality and safety of any welding and joints both for the columns and the pipework,

- the conventional fire insulation of those steel members which are connected to the water-cooled system, but are not directly water cooled.

5.4   Design examples

In the preceding chapters, only the basic features of the fire design of water filled SHS-columns have been given. Therefore, to give a complete example for the fire design of water filled columns would be outside the scope of this manual. Reference should be made to the appropriate, specialized literature, in particular [20]. However, additional design information and a simple partial design of a waterfilled structure is given in Annex III of this design guide.

6 Connections and fire resistance

6.1 Unfilled SHS-columns

The connections of both protected and unprotected steel structures normally have a lower local Shape Factor than the adjacent members and will, therefore attain lower steel temperatures.

Since neither in practice nor during fire tests has failure been initiated in a structure or a test element by the behaviour of connections, these can be designed using normal room temperature design codes.

However, when bolted connections are used for insulated steel members, care must be taken to ensure that the bolt heads and nuts are as well protected as the cleat. This will normally lead to a local increase of insulation thickness.

6.2 Concrete filled SHS-columns

Concrete filled hollow section columns generally fulfil fire protection requirements without further precautions. For economic reasons this construction method needs easily erectable connections between the columns and beams, which preferably should correspond to those of pure steel construction. Suitably designed connections will be fire resistant and can even improve the fire performance of the whole structure. However, the loads have to be transferred from the beams to the columns in such a way that all structural components – structural steel, reinforcement and concrete – contribute to the load bearing capacity according to their strength.

A well constructed column/beam-connection should:
- provide simple installation;
- optimize prefabrication of columns and beams;
- ensure adequate fire resistance without disturbing any external protective cladding.

If a building structure is braced (central core), the connections normally transfer shear loads only. In steel constructions two different types of connections between beams and columns are used:

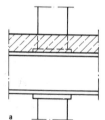 

Fig. 6.1 – Beam to column connection for continuous beams (a) and continuous columns (b); principle sketch

- for continuous beams (see Fig. 6.1a):
  The columns are connected to the beam by flanges, the shear forces are transferred to the columns by direct bearing on the column heads. Such connections can be classified to the same fire resistance category as the composite beams and columns without further design provisions.
- for continuous columns (see Fig. 6.1b):
  The connection of the beam to the columns is designed as a pinned joint. The shear forces are transferred to the columns by connection elements. To gain high fire resistance, these

elements can be protected, be over-designed or be specially designed, so that the forces can be transferred even though the material loses its strength under fire action. Two types of pinned joint connections have been investigated:

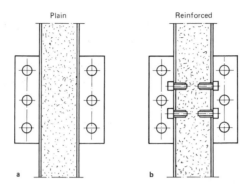

Fig. 6.2 – Beam to column connection with a "plain" (a) and a "reinforced" (b) cleat (a to be used only for low fire resistance requirements)

Connections, which have a vertically installed connecting cleat:

Although the cleats may be fastened to the steel section without any further precautions (Fig. 6.2a), it is recommended that part of the load is transferred to the concrete core by bolts or studs (see Fig. 6.2b) or by using a continuous cleat passed through the section (see Fig. 6.3). These measures guarantee the shear load transfer to the concrete and also prevent cleat rotation at the SHS wall, which may reduce the fire resistance of the adjacent beam. This load transfer must take place, whether the filled SHS-column is designed as a fully composite column under room temperature conditions or as an unprotected concrete filled column designed specifically to resist fire.

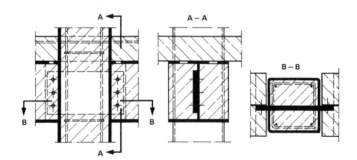

Fig. 6.3 – Beam to column connection with a cleat passed through the column.

Connections, where the beams are seated on brackets:

If the seating bracket is only welded to the hollow section of the composite column, the tube wall may buckle locally after some 20 minutes of fire action. This may lead, at least, to significant rotations of the bracket and, possibly, to the beam slipping off the bracket. Higher fire resistances can be gained if shear studs are welded on the back face of the bracket (Fig. 6.4). These are passed through holes of the hollow-section and embedded in the concrete of the column, so that the cleat is completely anchored under fire action.

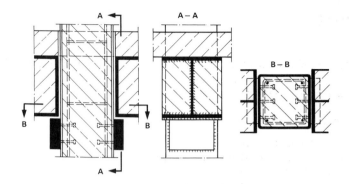

Fig. 6.4 – Beam to column connection with a support bracket for the beam

Both shear plate and shear stud design is based on room temperature design rules [16; 23]. Refer to Annex II for further background and a design example.

The design of rigid joints in combination with concrete filled SHS-columns is still under study. General design recommendations can therefore not be given.

6.3 Water filled SHS-columns

No experimental evidence is available for the performance of fire exposed connections in water filled steel structures. Nevertheless, by analogy to the behaviour of connections in unfilled SHS, one may presume that their behaviour is not critical and that no specific design measures are necessary. See also chapter 6.1.

7 Symbols

CEN   Comité Européen de Normalisation (European Committee for Standardisation)
EC   European Community or Eurocode
SHS   Structural Hollow Section

Upper case letters

A_c cross sectional area of concrete
A_m surface area of a steel member/unit length
A_r cross sectional area of reinforcement
A_s cross sectional area of steel hollow section
C   concrete grade (see diagrams I 1 to I 42)
E   fire resistance criterion with regard to integrity
I   fire resistance criterion with regard to insulation
$L_{cr,\theta}$ buckling length under fire conditions
M   maximum applied end moment
N   axial load
$N_{cr,\theta}$ buckling resistance under fire conditions
N_{eq} equivalent axial load
R   fire resistance criterion with regard to stability
   or   load bearing capacity
R_{Mpl} plastic moment of cross-section at room temperature
R_{nc} compression resistance of gross cross-section at room temperature
S   mechanical loading
V   volume of a steel member/unit length

Lower case letters

b   side length of a rectangular SHS
c   a correction factor used for columns to obtain the effective degree of utilization
d   diameter of a circular SHS
d_i thickness of external thermal insulation
d_r concrete cover to reinforcement
k   a moment modification factor (used in EC3 Part 1)
p_r percentage of reinforcement
r_j load bearing capacity in fire of a single component of a composite cross-section
t   time; wallthickness of steel hollow section
i   radius of gyration

Subscripts

fi   value relevent to the fire situation
fr   fire resistance
u   ultimate

Greek letters

θ temperature
θ_s steel temperature
θ_{crit} critical temperature
μ degree of utilization
X_{min} buckling coefficient according to curve "c" of EC3 Part 1 or any equivalent national
                buckling curve

8 References

[1] ISO: "Fire resistance tests – Elements of building construction", International Standard ISO 834, first edition, 1975.

[2] Underwriters Laboratory: "Fire Tests of Building Construction and Materials", UL 263, USA, 1991.

[3] IMO: "Recommendation on fire test procedure for "A", "B" and "F" class divisions", IMO Resolution A.517(13), November 1983.

[4] Eurocode 3: "Design of Steel Structures – Part 1.2: Structural fire design"; Draft prENV 1993-1-2, May 1993.

[5] Eurocode 4: "Design of Composite Steel and Concrete Structures – Part 1.2: Structural Fire Design", Draft prENV 1993-1-2, January 1993.

[6] Steel Promotion Committee of Eurofer: "Steel and fire safety: a global approach", Eurofer, Brussels, 1990.

[7] Eurocode 2: "Design of Concrete Structures – Part 10: Structural fire design of concrete structures", final draft, Luxembourg, April 1990.

[8] Twilt, L. and Both, C.: "Technical Notes on the Realistic Behaviour and Design of Fire Exposed Steel and Composite Structures", Final Report ECSC 7210 SA112, Activity D: "Basis for Technical Notes", TNO Building and Construction Research, BI-91-069, 1991.

[9] Eurocode 1: "Basis of Design and Actions on Structures – Part 2.7: Actions on Structures Exposed to Fire", Draft ENV 1993.

[10] Eurocode 3: "Design of Steel Structures – Part 1.1: General Rules and Rules for Buildings", ENV 1993.

[11] CEFICOSS: "Computer Engineering of the Fire resistance for Composite and Steel Structures", Computer code for both thermal and mechanical response of steel and composite structures exposed to fire, ARBED, Luxembourg.

[12] COMSYS-T: Computer code for the determination of the ultimate load bearing capacity in fire case, Wuppertal University, Institute for Structural Engineering and Fire Safety, Germany.

[13] STABA-F: Computer code for the determination of load bearing and deformation behaviour of uni-axial structural elements (beams, columns) under fire action, Technical University of Brunswick, Germany.

[14] DIANA: "DIsplacement method ANAlyser", A general purpose finite element programme, suitable for the calculation of geometrical and physical non linear problems, TNO Building and Construction Research, The Netherlands.

[15] Klingsch, W.: "Optimization of Cross Sections of Steel Composite Columns", Proceedings of the third International Conference on Steel-Concrete Composite Structures, Fukuoka, Japan, p. 99-105, 1991.

[16] Eurocode 4: "Design of composite steel and concrete structures – Part 1 – General Rules and Rules for Buildings", Luxembourg, Revised draft, issue 1, October, 1990.

[17] Grandjean, G., Grimault, J.-P., and Petit, L.: "Détermination de la Durée au Feu des Profiles Creux Remplis de Béton", Cometube, 1980 (also published as ECSC-report no. 7210 SA3/302).

[18] Twilt, L., and Haar, v.d. P. W..: "Harmonization of the Calculation Rules for the Fire Resistance of Concrete Filled SHS-columns". CIDECT-project 15F-86/7-0; IBBC-TNO report B-86-461, August 1986.

[19] Twilt, L.: "Design Charts for the Fire Resistance of Concrete Filled HSS columns under Centric Loading", Final report CIDECT project 15J, TNO-report BI-88-134, August 1988.

[20] EN YYY5: "Methods of Test for the Contribution to Fire Resistance of Structural Member: Part 4B: Applied Protection to Concrete Filled Hollow Steel Columns".

[21] Hönig, O., Klingsch, W., Witte, H.: "Baulicher Brandschutz durch wassergefüllte Stützen in Rahmentragwerken (Fire Resistance of Water Filled Columns)", Research Report, Studiengesellschaft für Stahlanwendung e.V., Düsseldorf, Forschungsbericht p. 86/4.5, 1985.

[22] Bond, G. V. L.: "Fire and steel construction, Water cooled hollow columns", Constrado, Croydon, 1975.

[23] Roik, K., Bergmann, R., Haensel, J., and Hanswille, G.: "Verbundkonstruktionen, Bemessung auf der Grundlage des Eurocode 4, Teil 1", Betonkalender, Verlag für Architektur und technische Wissenschaften, Ernst & Sohn, Berlin, 1993.

9 Building examples

Germany: Gobaplan Building System

A typical office building system using square steel hollow sections is Gobaplan. It can be up to five storeys high, with a variable ground plan based on a 2.40 m module. The storey heights can be varied from about 3.0 m to more than 3.40 m. The load bearing structure uses 100 mm square steel hollow sections for the columns and small open H-sections for the beams. The wall panels and floor slabs are made of prefabricated concrete elements. The fire requirements up to 90 minutes are fulfilled by using suspended ceilings to protect the beams and also using the combined effect of plaster boards with the wall units as an integrated system to protect the columns. This leads to a most competitive design because of low costs and speedy erection.

Steel workshop: Goldbeckbau GmbH,
Bielefeld
Fire engineer: Hosser, Hass + Partner,
Brunswick

Germany: Hanover Norcon Building

The hanging offices of Hanover are a five storey building. The ground floor, which is not directly connected with the statically loaded system of the main building, is suspended at a distance of about one meter above ground level over the full floor area. Each of the four upper storeys is suspended on a water cooled hanger fixed to the main girder at the top of the building. The girder itself hangs under the top of the main load bearing column group. Each of the columns is a water cooled system.

Both the hangers and the columns are of tubular design with a CIP water cooling system.

Each group of four columns and each group of hangers has its own water storage tank at the top. Ninety minutes fire resistance was required. However, by refilling the system, unlimited fire resistance of the cooled steel structure is possible.

No additional fire insulation is necessary for the water cooled steel structure.

Columns: 470 $\varnothing$ × 25 + 216 $\varnothing$ × 6
Hangers: 121 $\varnothing$ × 10 + 42.4 $\varnothing$ × 2.6

Architect: SE-Architekten Schuwirth and Erman, Hanover
Workshop: Krupp Stahlbau, Hanover
Fire Engineer: HWK – Honig, Klingsch, Witte, Wiesbaden/Remscheid

The Netherlands: Amsterdam Mees Lease Building

This four storey office building with an 1820 m² floor area has been built with a steel structure, up to now, not very common in The Netherlands. In comparison with a traditional concrete structure, the steel structure was 10% cheaper, much lighter and quicker to erect.

The steel structure is a braced frame with tubular columns and integrated beams supporting concrete hollow core slabs.

A one hour fire resistance was required. This could be easily achieved on the basis of the CIDECT design rules by filling the 323 dia. CHS columns with concrete and by the integrated HEA beams that are embedded in concrete. Thus, no additional fire insulation was necessary for this building.

Architect: J & S Architects B.V., Boxtel
Structural Engineer: ECCS B.V., Hillegom and P. de Jong, Amsterdam
Fire Engineer: Idem
Steel Fabricator: Evers Staalkonstrukties Hillegom B.V., Hillegom
Main Contractor: IBB-Kondor Leiden B.V., Leiden

United Kingdom: Darlington Memorial Hospital

RHS filled with concrete was adopted for the internal columns of the 8 and 9 storey development for the Darlington Memorial Hospital so as to give the most compact columns to suit the module of the "Tartan" grid arrangement.

The building has a plan of 94 × 48 m and a maximum height of 33 m. The lower three floors have twin columns of 150 × 150 mm RHS, filled with concrete with a 28 day cube strength of 60 N/mm^2. Higher levels have single columns of 203.2 × 152.4 RHS filled with 30 N/mm^2 concrete. All the RHS sections are according to BS 4360 50C.

The columns were erected in three storey lengths and were filled with concrete after the construction of the concrete floor slab at the top of each column length. Column connections were made with bolted flanges at floor level.

Fire resistance required was 1 hour, except in the basement level storage area, where 1.5 hours were required. Fire resistance was provided by encasing the columns with 38 mm of vermiculite plaster after construction. No account was taken on the benefical effects of concrete filling in determining fire prevention thickness requirements.

United Kingdom: Rochdale Bus Station

RHS columns, 150 mm square and 3.3 m high, were filled with steel fibre reinforced concrete after erection to provide compact columns of 1 hour fire resistance without the need for external casing. The columns support the floor of the bus crew rest room/canteen above the public areas of the bus station. A standard fire resistance test to BS 476: Part 8 was carried out on a representative column to demonstrate that adequate fire resistance was achieved.

Architects: Essex, Goodman and Suggit
Consulting Engineers: De Leuw, Chadwick, Oheocha
Main Contractor: John Laing Construction Ltd.

Finland: The Tecnocent building, Oulu

The Tecnocent building is situated in Oulu science park. The purpose of the building is to serve the companies that do research, develop and produce high-tech products. Because of its high-tech image, steel was used in the bearing structures and also in the facades and composite floors.
The bearing columns consist of both circular (diameter 219 mm) and square (200 × 200 mm) sections. The fire resistance requirement was 60 minutes. This requirement was fulfilled by filling the hollow sections with concrete using reinforcement bars. This is a widely used fire protection method in Finland. Concrete filling of the sections was done in the steel workshop. This was possible because both the steel workshop and the concrete factory were very near to the building site.

Architects: Architects J & J, Oy, Oulu
Engineering office: Poysala & Sandberg Oy, Oulu
Steel workshop: Oy Oulun Hypoco, Oulu

51

Finland: Tampere, Lapinniemi Building

The Lapinniemi Building is an old factory building which was built in 1897. The building was restored in 1989 – 1990 to be used as residences as well as bathing establishment. The old construction used mainly bricks and cast iron. The new construction is made of CHS sections and is architectonically suited to the old parts of the building.

Since the use of this building had been changed, the fire requirements had also to be re-assessed. In the beginning of the century, there were no requirements for the steel parts to resist fire. After the renovation, all steel elements of the structure had to fulfil a 60 minutes fire resistance requirement. Because the building was partly old and partly new, the most suitable fire protection method was fire resistant paint. An important advantage was also gained, as the beautiful old cast iron columns were not hidden by the fire protection material.

Steel workshop:	Teräselementti Oy
Architect:	AR-Tsto Antti Katajamäki Ky
Engineering Office for steel constructions:	TE-EM-Oy

Australia: Riverside Office Building, Adelaide

The Riverside Office Building's basic shape is composed of four octagonal "pods", surrounding a central atrium. Each pod is approximately 550 square metres in area. A typical pod floor layout consists of primary composite beams orientated at 45 degrees to the column grid. Columns are circular, reinforced, concrete filled steel tubes. Lateral forces from earthquake and wind are resisted by a combination of a tubular steel K-frame bracing system located around the perimeter of the atrium core and circular concrete stair cores located on the east and west sides of the building. The lift shafts are centrally located within the atrium and are fully welded rectangular hollow section steel frames, not fire protected.

The columns are required to have 120 minutes resistance to fire. Under normal conditions, the concrete and the steel act compositely; but in a fire the reinforced concrete section of the column carries the load. The exposed tubular K-bracing system is not fire rated since the external concrete stair cores provide the lateral stability during a fire. However, the bracing is considered fully effective when resisting earthquakes and wind.

Columns (general):   600 mm diameter
Columns (lift shaft): RHS 152 × 152 mm
K-Brace Diagonals: CHS ∅ 406 × 6.3 mm

Architects: John Andrews International Pty Ltd., Sydney and Woodhead Hall McDonald Shaw Pty Ltd., Adelaide
Structural Engineer: Pak Poy & Kneebone Pty Ltd., Adelaide
Builder: Hansen Yuncken (S.A.) Pty Ltd.

France: Microsoft Head Office, Villebon-sur-Yvette

Located in a business park, the Microsoft Head Office had to express through its design the vitality of the corporation. This is achieved by using simple means. Built around five interior gardens with a view to create an efficient linking system between the different departments of the Microsoft organization, the complex consists of two- and three-storey structures. The simplest steel frame possible is designed for the whole structure. Since the fire protection for the horizontal structure is hidden by a suspended ceiling, its appearance is not important. However, in order to keep the vertical structure visible, a variety of tubular columns filled with concrete have been applied ($\square$ 250 × 250 mm). The required fire resistance is 60 minutes.

Architect: Paul Depondt, Cergy
Developer: Innovation Immobliere, Nanterre
Structural Engineer: Themis Constantindis, Boulogne
Steel workshop: Entreprise Barbot, Descartes

Japan: Mitsui Soko Hakozaki Building
(High rise residential building)

This high-rise residential building (76 units) which stands on the bank of the Sumida River located in the centre of Tokyo has 19 storeys above the ground and a total floor area of 9,006 m². The structural frame is composed of concrete filled tubular (CFT) steel columns and steel framed reinforced concrete beams, both of which were made by the site prefabrication method. Each side of the square shaped CFT column is 600 mm. The CFT columns were made by filling each two storey length with concrete (strength of 27 Mpa) at the site.

By concrete filling, the thickness of the fire resistance covering of each CFT column could be reduced by 30 – 50% compared to the thickness of covering materials for a similar empty steel column.

Architect: Takenaka Corporation
Structural Engineer: Takenaka Corporation
Fire Engineer: Takenaka Corporation
Contractor: Takenaka Corporation

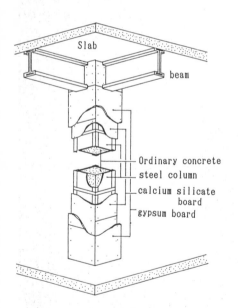

Japan: Nakanoshima Intes

This office building, which stands at Nakanoshima in the centre of Osaka City, has one basement, 22 storeys above ground and a total floor area of 24,770 m². The structural frame is composed of concrete filled tubular (CFT) columns and steel beams. The square CFT columns have a side length of 600 – 850 mm and the circular CFT columns have diameters between 700 – 800 mm. The columns were filled with concrete at the factory. An empirical and analytical investigation was carried out to estimate the fire resistance of these CFT columns based on the results of the study of the "New Urban Housing Project", which was carried out under the leadership of the Ministry of Construction. From the results of the investigation, it was verified that the CFT columns used for the 10th floor up to the 22nd floor (for which 60 – 120 minutes are required according to the Japanese fire resistance rating rules) did not need to be covered with fire resistant materials. The construction of the building was subsequently executed with the approval of the Ministry of Construction.

Architect: Takenaka Corporation
Structural Engineer: Takenaka Corporation
Fire Engineer: Takenaka Corporation

Japan: ENICOM Computer Centre

This building, with 6 storeys and a total floor area of 10,960 m², was constructed in Tokyo. As the building is intended for computer facilities, concrete filled steel rectangular columns (600 mm sq. × 19 mm thick) were adopted to prevent excessive structural vibration (seismic isolators were also adopted). By using Fire Resistant steel, the thickness of the fire protection (a ceramics-type sprayed material) needed to fulfil the required 2 hours fire resistance was reduced to 5 mm (the required thickness for conventional steel was 30 mm). This also removed the need to use a layer of reinforcement within the protection layer.

Architect: Nippon Steel Corp.
Structural Engineer: Nippon Steel Corp.
                        and Tokyo Structural
                        Engineers
Fire Engineer: Nippon Steel Corp.
Main Contractor: Nippon Steel Corp.

Annex I: Design graphs for unprotected concrete filled SHS-columns

Table I.1

Fire Class	Concrete Grade	Section Size	Diagram No.
R 60 R 90 R 120	C 20	⌀ 219.1 × 4.5	I 1 I 2 I 3
R 60 R 90 R 120		⌀ 244.5 × 5.0	I 4 I 5 I 6
R 60 R 90 R 120	C 30	⌀ 273.0 × 5.0	I 7 I 8 I 9
R 60 R 90 R 120		⌀ 323.9 × 5.6	I 10 I 11 I 12
R 60 R 90 R 120	C 40	⌀ 355.6 × 5.6	I 13 I 14 I 15
R 60 R 90 R 120		⌀ 406.4 × 6.3	I 16 I 17 I 18
R 30 R 60 R 90	C 20	□ 180 × 6.3	I 19 I 20 I 21
R 30 R 60 R 90		□ 200 × 6.3	I 22 I 23 I 24
R 30 R 60 R 90		□ 220 × 6.3	I 25 I 26 I 27
R 60 R 90 R 120	C 30	□ 250 × 6.3	I 28 I 29 I 30
R 60 R 90 R 120		□ 260 × 6.3	I 31 I 32 I 33
R 60 R 90 R 120	C 40	□ 300 × 7.1	I 34 I 35 I 36
R 60 R 90 R 120		□ 350 × 8.0	I 37 I 38 I 39
R 60 R 90 R 120		□ 400 × 10.0	I 40 I 41 I 42

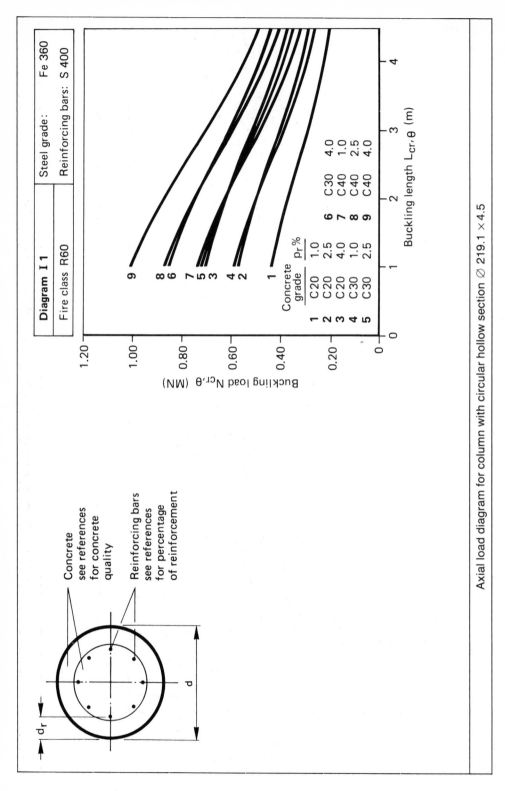

Axial load diagram for column with circular hollow section ⌀ 219.1 × 4.5

60

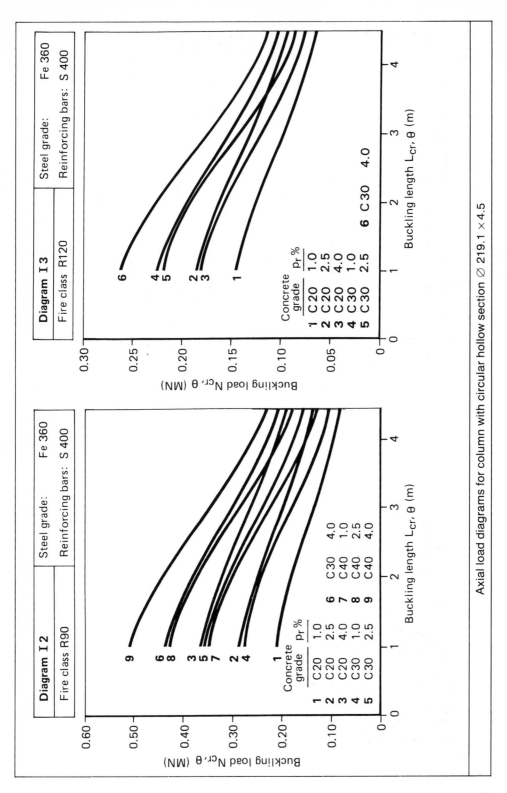

Axial load diagrams for column with circular hollow section ∅ 219.1 × 4.5

Diagram I 3

| Steel grade: | Fe 360 |
| Fire class R120 | Reinforcing bars: S 400 |

	Concrete grade	p_r %
1	C20	1.0
2	C20	2.5
3	C20	4.0
4	C30	1.0
5	C30	2.5
6	C30	4.0

Buckling length $L_{cr, \theta}$ (m)

Buckling load $N_{cr, \theta}$ (MN)

Diagram I 2

| Steel grade: | Fe 360 |
| Fire class R90 | Reinforcing bars: S 400 |

	Concrete grade	p_r %			
1	C20	1.0	6	C30	4.0
2	C20	2.5	7	C40	1.0
3	C20	4.0	8	C40	2.5
4	C30	1.0	9	C40	4.0
5	C30	2.5			

Buckling length $L_{cr, \theta}$ (m)

Buckling load $N_{cr, \theta}$ (MN)

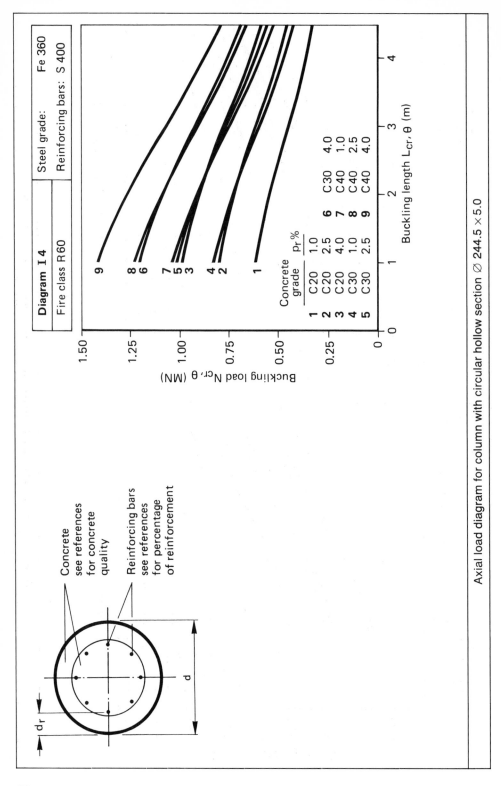

Axial load diagram for column with circular hollow section ⌀ 244.5 × 5.0

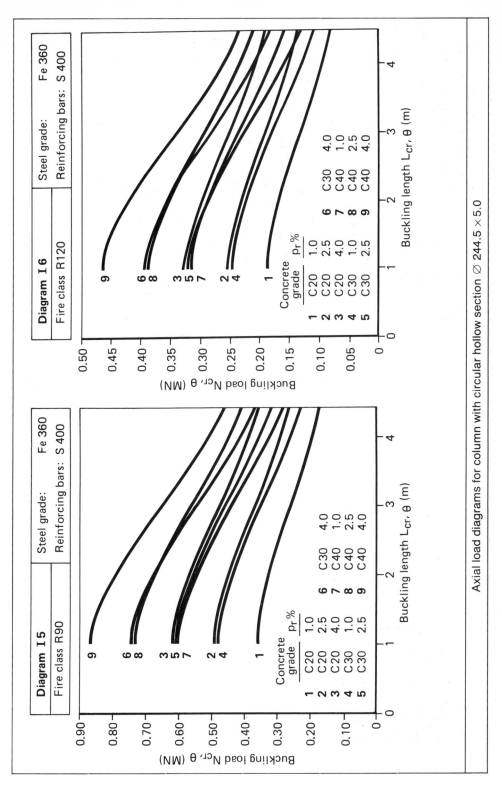

Axial load diagrams for column with circular hollow section ∅ 244.5 × 5.0

63

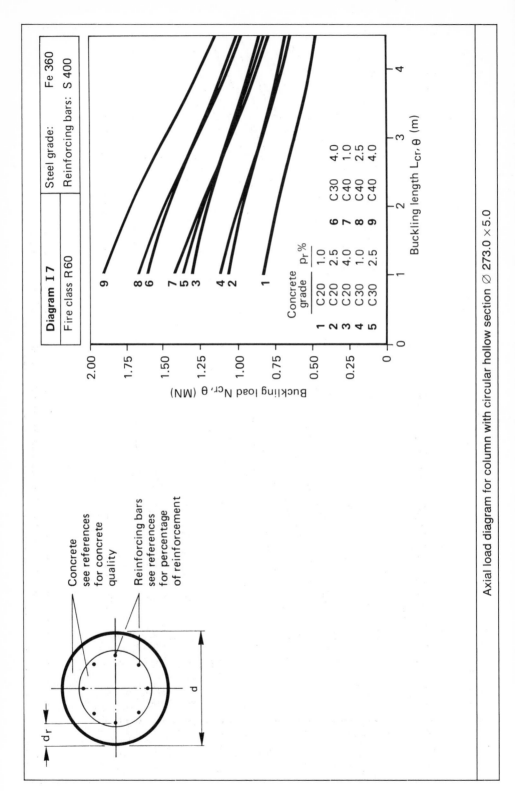

Axial load diagram for column with circular hollow section ⌀ 273.0 × 5.0

64

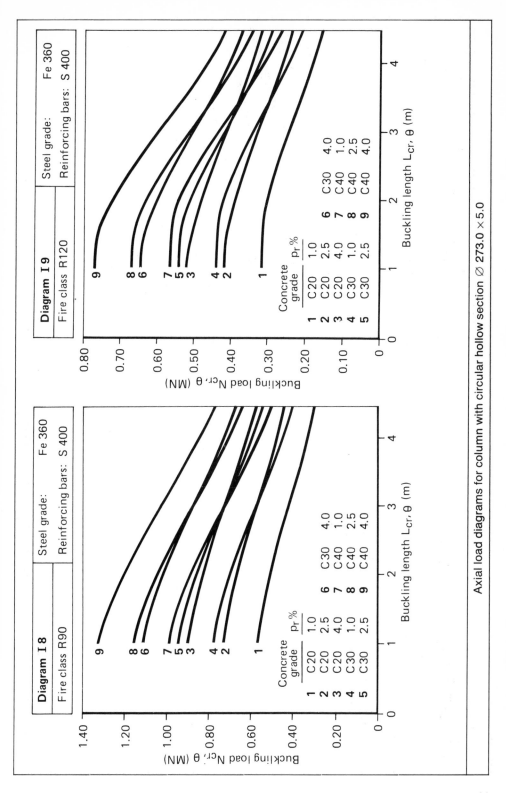

Axial load diagrams for column with circular hollow section ∅ 273.0 × 5.0

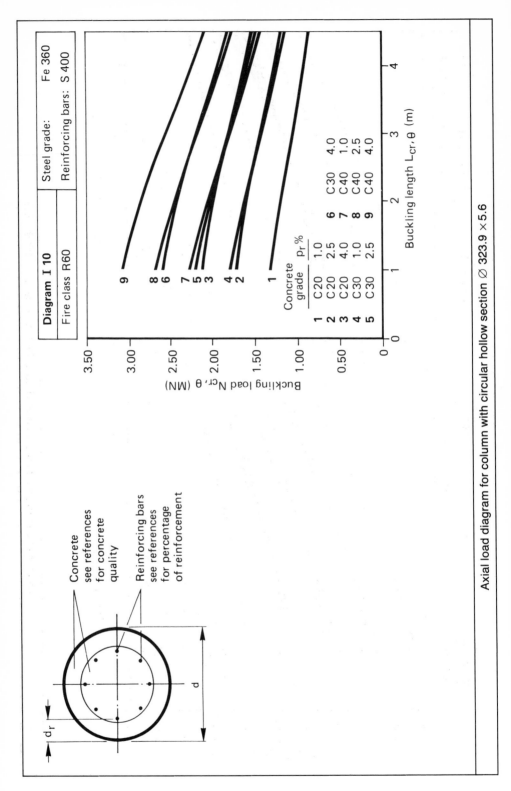

Axial load diagram for column with circular hollow section ∅ 323.9 × 5.6

Diagram I 10

Steel grade:	Fe 360
Reinforcing bars:	S 400

Fire class R60

	Concrete grade	p_r %			Concrete grade	p_r %
1	C20	1.0	**6**	C30	4.0
2	C20	2.5	**7**	C40	1.0
3	C20	4.0	**8**	C40	2.5
4	C30	1.0	**9**	C40	4.0
5	C30	2.5			

Buckling load $N_{cr,\theta}$ (MN)

Buckling length $L_{cr,\theta}$ (m)

Concrete
see references
for concrete
quality

Reinforcing bars
see references
for percentage
of reinforcement

d

d_r

66

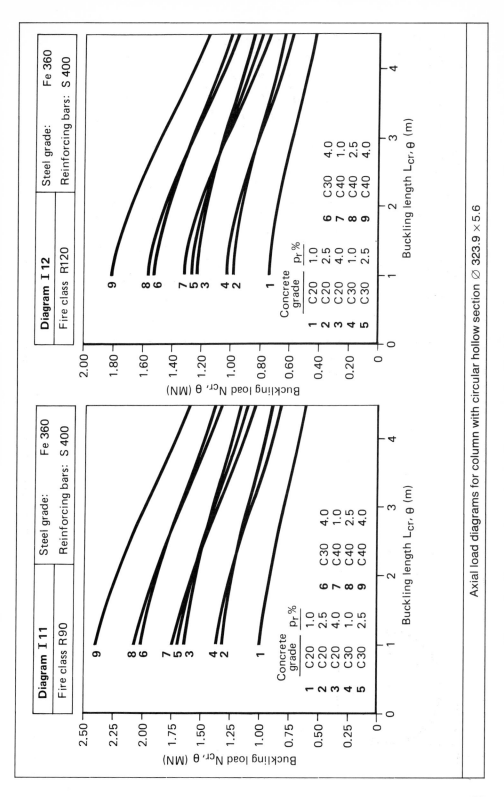

Axial load diagrams for column with circular hollow section ⌀ 323.9 × 5.6

67

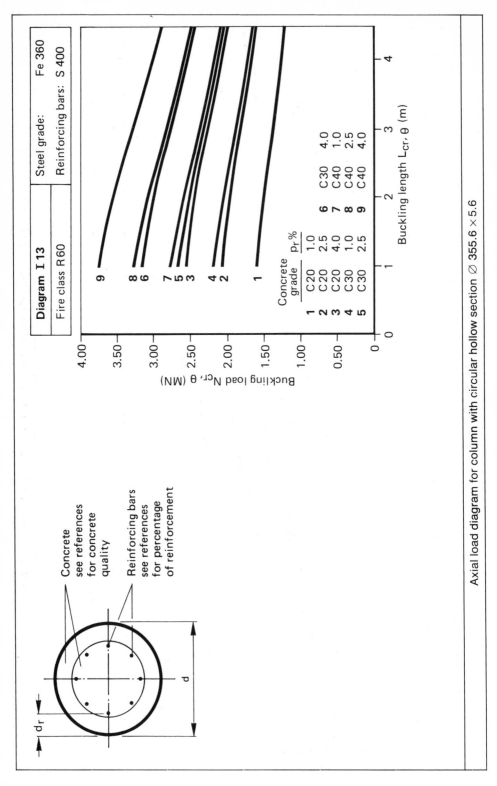

Axial load diagram for column with circular hollow section ⌀ 355.6 × 5.6

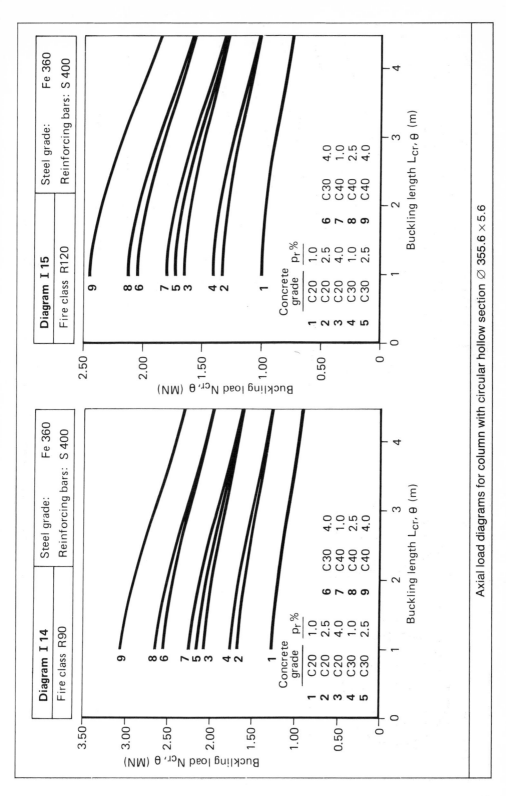

Axial load diagrams for column with circular hollow section ∅ 355.6 × 5.6

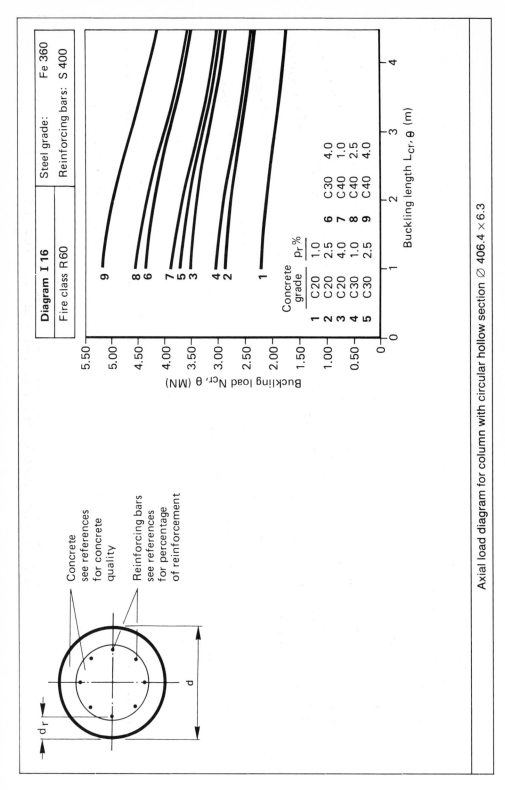

Axial load diagram for column with circular hollow section ⌀ 406.4 × 6.3

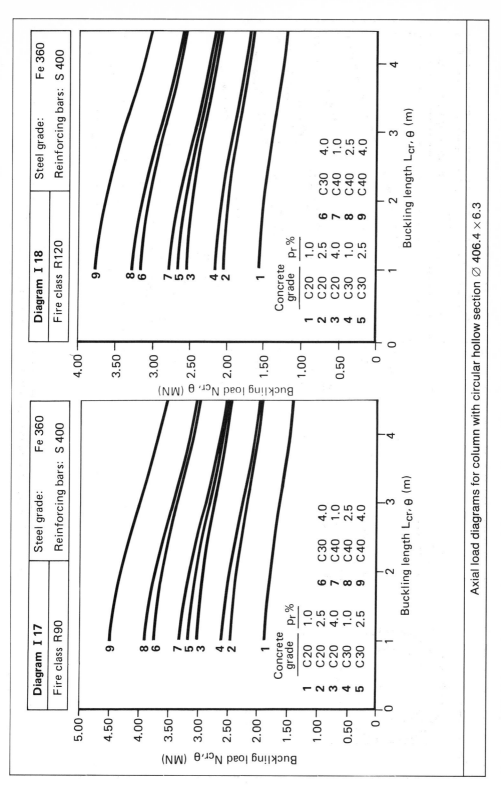

Axial load diagrams for column with circular hollow section $\varnothing$ 406.4 $\times$ 6.3

71

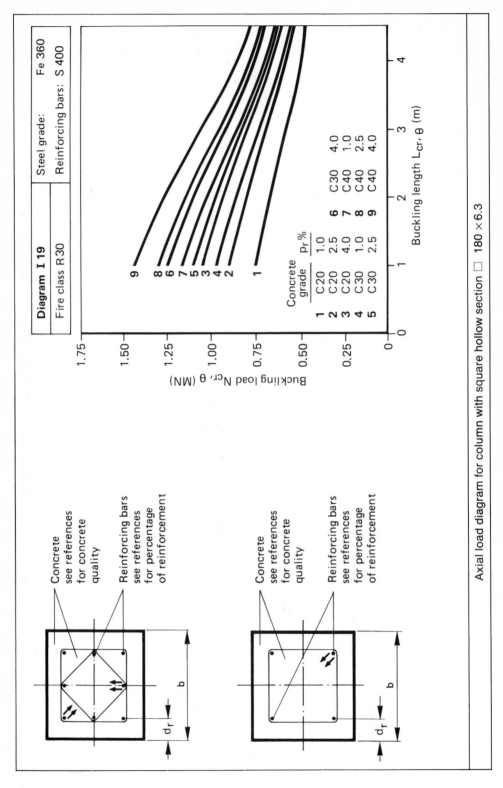

Axial load diagram for column with square hollow section □ 180 × 6.3

72

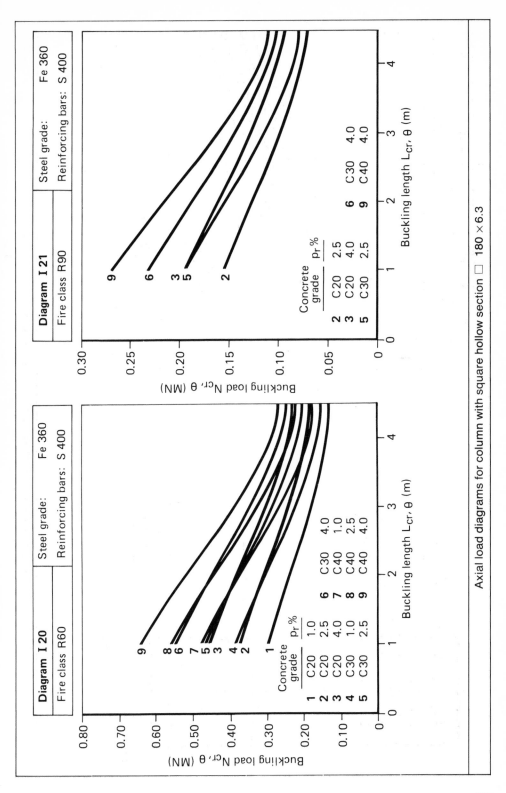

Axial load diagrams for column with square hollow section ☐ 180 × 6.3

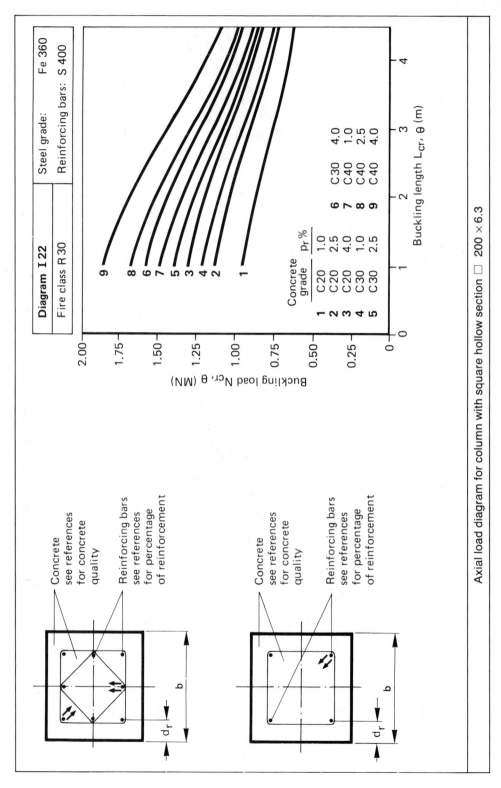

Diagram I 22

Fire class R 30

| Steel grade: | Fe 360 |
| Reinforcing bars: | S 400 |

Concrete grade		pr %
1	C20	1.0
2	C20	2.5
3	C20	4.0
4	C30	1.0
5	C30	2.5
6	C30	4.0
7	C40	1.0
8	C40	2.5
9	C40	4.0

Buckling load $N_{cr, \theta}$ (MN)

Buckling length $L_{cr, \theta}$ (m)

Concrete
see references
for concrete
quality

Reinforcing bars
see references
for percentage
of reinforcement

Concrete
see references
for concrete
quality

Reinforcing bars
see references
for percentage
of reinforcement

Axial load diagram for column with square hollow section □ 200 × 6.3

74

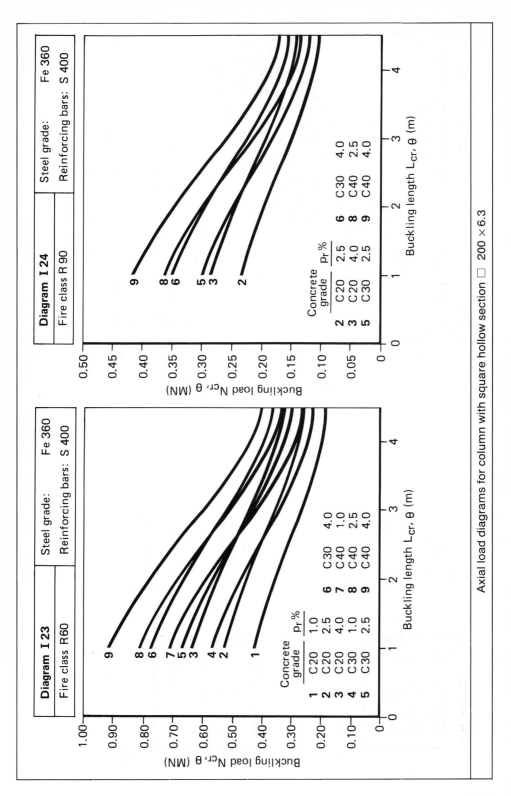

Diagram I 23

Steel grade:	Fe 360
Reinforcing bars:	S 400

Fire class R60

Buckling length $L_{cr, \theta}$ (m)

Buckling load $N_{cr, \theta}$ (MN)

	Concrete grade	p_r %				
1	C20	1.0	**6**	C30	4.0
2	C20	2.5	**7**	C40	1.0
3	C20	4.0	**8**	C40	2.5
4	C30	1.0	**9**	C40	4.0
5	C30	2.5			

Diagram I 24

Steel grade:	Fe 360
Reinforcing bars:	S 400

Fire class R 90

Buckling length $L_{cr, \theta}$ (m)

Buckling load $N_{cr, \theta}$ (MN)

	Concrete grade	p_r %				
2	C20	2.5	**6**	C30	4.0
3	C20	4.0	**8**	C40	2.5
5	C30	2.5	**9**	C40	4.0

Axial load diagrams for column with square hollow section □ 200 × 6.3

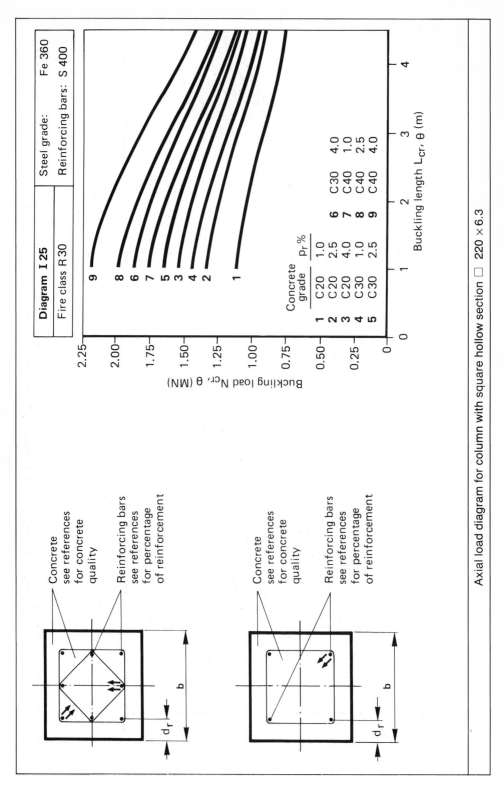

Diagram I 25

Steel grade:	Fe 360
Reinforcing bars:	S 400

Fire class R 30

Buckling load $N_{cr, \theta}$ (MN)

Buckling length $L_{cr, \theta}$ (m)

	Concrete grade	p_r %
1	C20	1.0
2	C20	2.5
3	C20	4.0
4	C30	1.0
5	C30	2.5
6	C30	4.0
7	C40	1.0
8	C40	2.5
9	C40	4.0

Concrete
see references
for concrete
quality

Reinforcing bars
see references
for percentage
of reinforcement

Concrete
see references
for concrete
quality

Reinforcing bars
see references
for percentage
of reinforcement

Axial load diagram for column with square hollow section □ 220 × 6.3

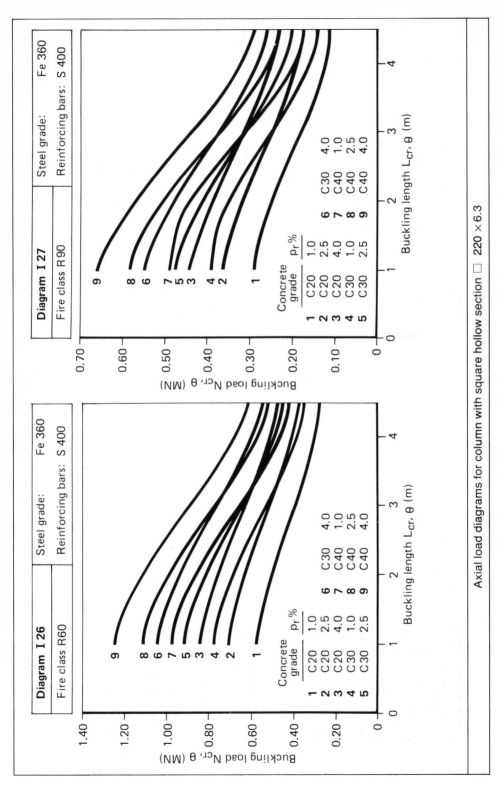

Axial load diagrams for column with square hollow section □ 220 × 6.3

Diagram I 26

Steel grade:	Fe 360
Reinforcing bars:	S 400

Fire class R60

	Concrete grade	p_r %
1	C20	1.0
2	C20	2.5
3	C20	4.0
4	C30	1.0
5	C30	2.5
6	C30	4.0
7	C40	1.0
8	C40	2.5
9	C40	4.0

Buckling length $L_{cr, \theta}$ (m)

Buckling load $N_{cr, \theta}$ (MN)

Diagram I 27

Steel grade:	Fe 360
Reinforcing bars:	S 400

Fire class R90

	Concrete grade	p_r %
1	C20	1.0
2	C20	2.5
3	C20	4.0
4	C30	1.0
5	C30	2.5
6	C30	4.0
7	C40	1.0
8	C40	2.5
9	C40	4.0

Buckling length $L_{cr, \theta}$ (m)

Buckling load $N_{cr, \theta}$ (MN)

77

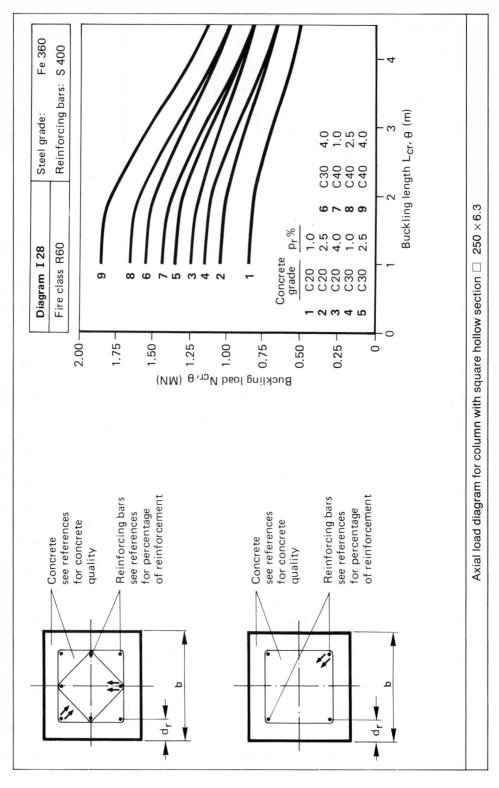

Axial load diagram for column with square hollow section □ 250 × 6.3

Diagram I 28

Fire class R60

Steel grade: Fe 360

Reinforcing bars: S 400

Buckling load $N_{cr, \theta}$ (MN)

Buckling length $L_{cr, \theta}$ (m)

Concrete grade	p_r %			
1	C20	1.0		
2	C20	2.5	**6** C30	4.0
3	C20	4.0	**7** C40	1.0
4	C30	1.0	**8** C40	2.5
5	C30	2.5	**9** C40	4.0

Concrete see references for concrete quality

Reinforcing bars see references for percentage of reinforcement

Concrete see references for concrete quality

Reinforcing bars see references for percentage of reinforcement

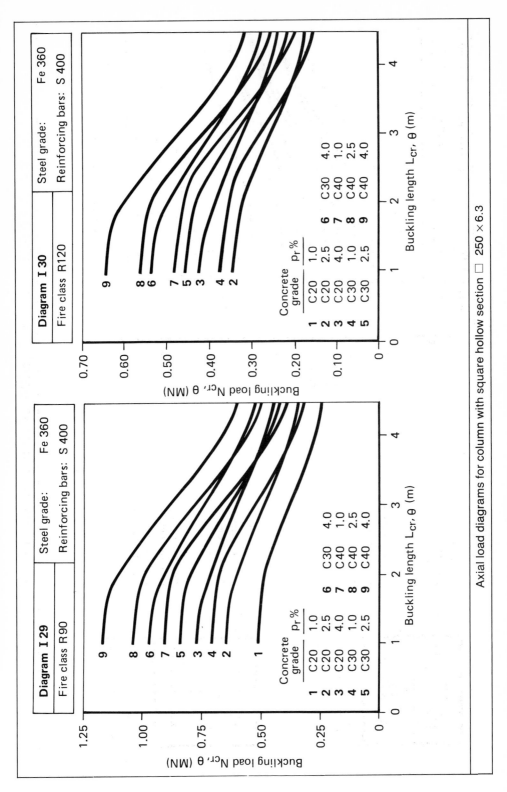

Diagram I 29	Steel grade:	Fe 360
Fire class R90	Reinforcing bars:	S 400

Concrete grade	p_r %			
1	C20	1.0	**6**	C30	4.0
2	C20	2.5	**7**	C40	1.0
3	C20	4.0	**8**	C40	2.5
4	C30	1.0	**9**	C40	4.0
5	C30	2.5			

Buckling length L_{cr}, θ (m)

Buckling load N_{cr}, θ (MN)

Diagram I 30	Steel grade:	Fe 360
Fire class R120	Reinforcing bars:	S 400

Concrete grade	p_r %			
1	C20	1.0	**6**	C30	4.0
2	C20	2.5	**7**	C40	1.0
3	C20	4.0	**8**	C40	2.5
4	C30	1.0	**9**	C40	4.0
5	C30	2.5			

Buckling length L_{cr}, θ (m)

Buckling load N_{cr}, θ (MN)

Axial load diagrams for column with square hollow section □ 250 × 6.3

79

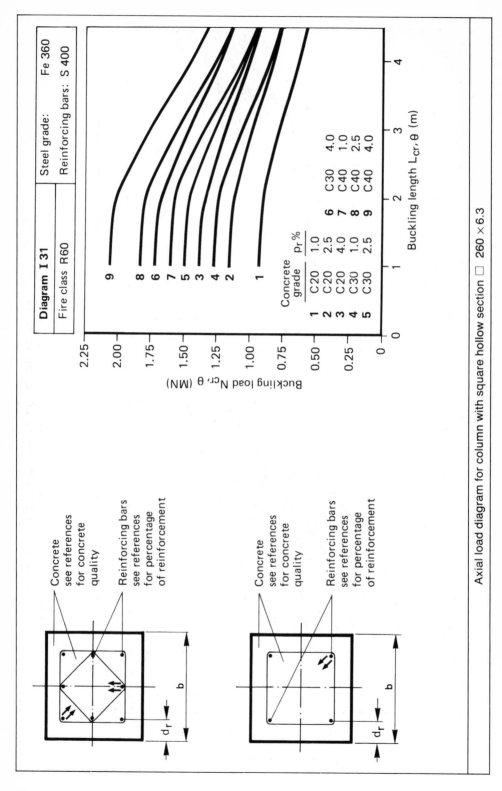

Axial load diagram for column with square hollow section ☐ 260 × 6.3

80

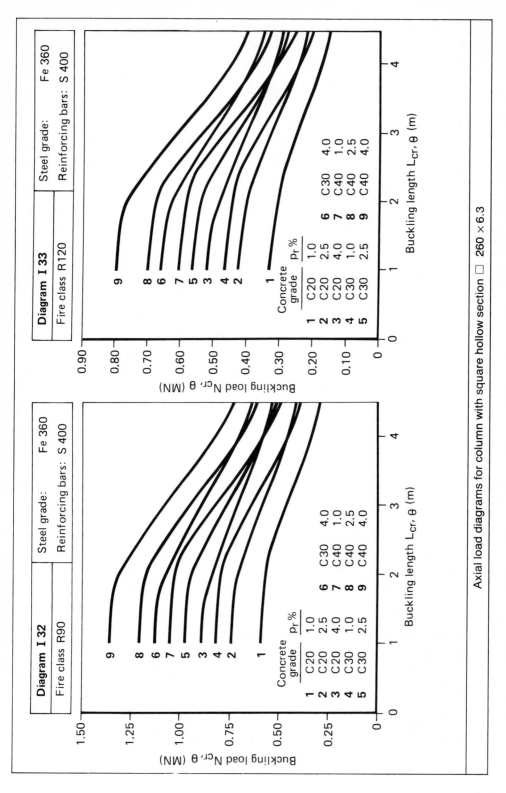

Diagram I 32

Steel grade:	Fe 360
Reinforcing bars:	S 400

Fire class R90

Concrete grade	p_r %
1 C20	1.0
2 C20	2.5
3 C20	4.0
4 C30	1.0
5 C30	2.5
6 C30	4.0
7 C40	1.0
8 C40	2.5
9 C40	4.0

Buckling length $L_{cr, \theta}$ (m)

Buckling load $N_{cr, \theta}$ (MN)

Diagram I 33

Steel grade:	Fe 360
Reinforcing bars:	S 400

Fire class R120

Concrete grade	p_r %
1 C20	1.0
2 C20	2.5
3 C20	4.0
4 C30	1.0
5 C30	2.5
6 C30	4.0
7 C40	1.0
8 C40	2.5
9 C40	4.0

Buckling length $L_{cr, \theta}$ (m)

Buckling load $N_{cr, \theta}$ (MN)

Axial load diagrams for column with square hollow section □ 260 × 6.3

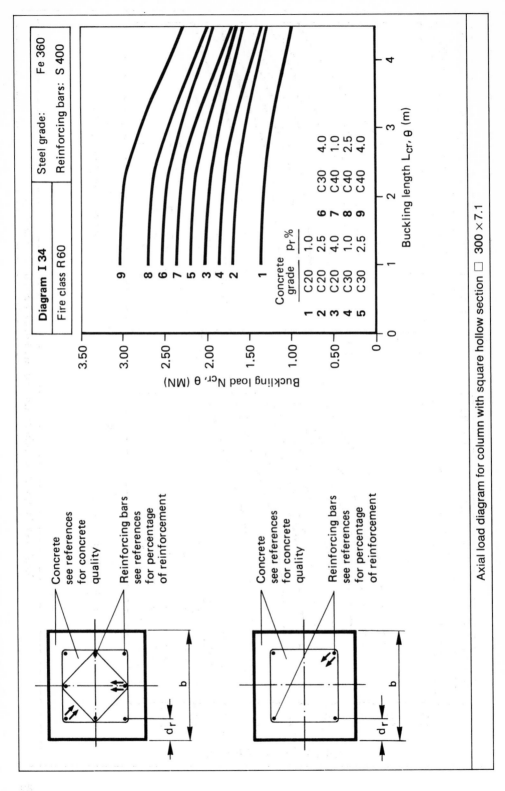

Diagram I 34	Steel grade:	Fe 360
Fire class R60	Reinforcing bars:	S 400

Buckling load $N_{cr, \theta}$ (MN)

Buckling length $L_{cr, \theta}$ (m)

	Concrete grade	p_r %			
1	C20	1.0	6	C30	4.0
2	C20	2.5	7	C40	1.0
3	C20	4.0	8	C40	2.5
4	C30	1.0	9	C40	4.0
5	C30	2.5			

Concrete
see references
for concrete
quality

Reinforcing bars
see references
for percentage
of reinforcement

Concrete
see references
for concrete
quality

Reinforcing bars
see references
for percentage
of reinforcement

Axial load diagram for column with square hollow section ☐ 300 × 7.1

82

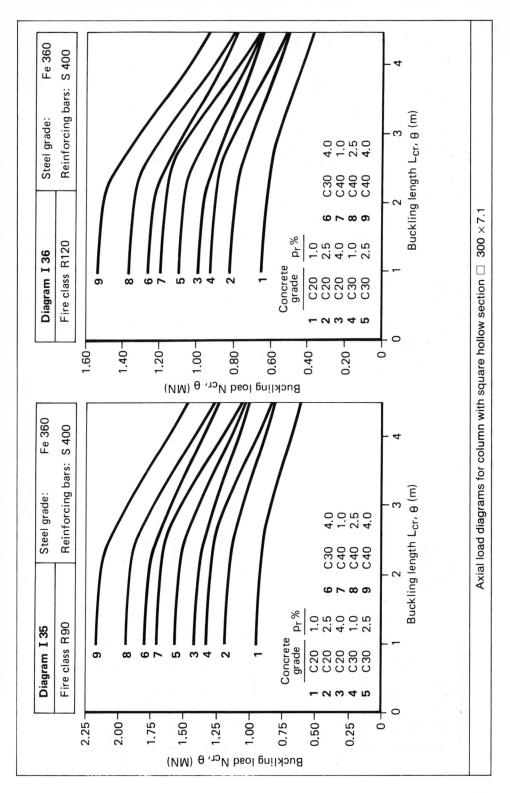

Axial load diagrams for column with square hollow section □ 300 × 7.1

83

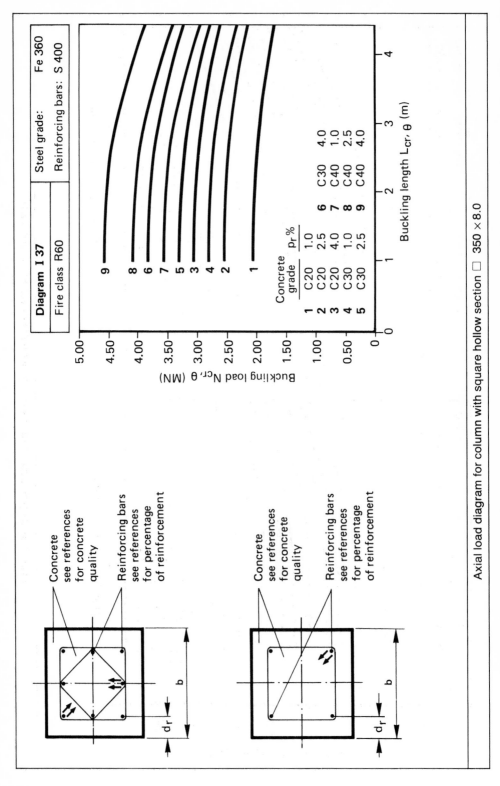

Axial load diagram for column with square hollow section □ 350 × 8.0

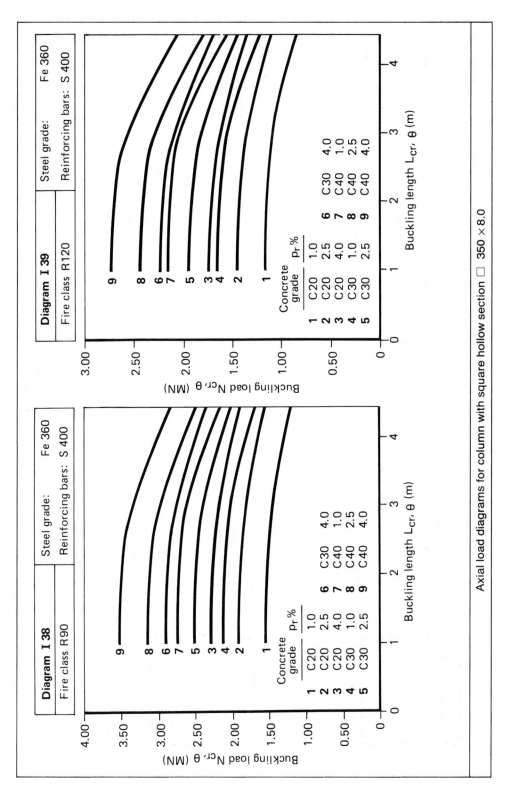

Axial load diagrams for column with square hollow section □ 350 × 8.0

Diagram I 38

| Steel grade: | Fe 360 |
| Reinforcing bars: | S 400 |

Fire class R90

	Concrete grade	p_r %				
1	C20	1.0	**6**	C30	4.0
2	C20	2.5	**7**	C40	1.0
3	C20	4.0	**8**	C40	2.5
4	C30	1.0	**9**	C40	4.0
5	C30	2.5			

Diagram I 39

| Steel grade: | Fe 360 |
| Reinforcing bars: | S 400 |

Fire class R120

	Concrete grade	p_r %				
1	C20	1.0	**6**	C30	4.0
2	C20	2.5	**7**	C40	1.0
3	C20	4.0	**8**	C40	2.5
4	C30	1.0	**9**	C40	4.0
5	C30	2.5			

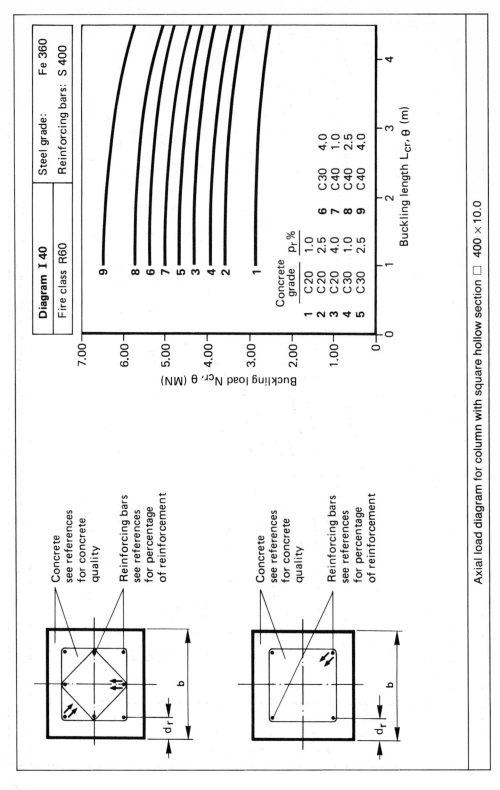

Axial load diagram for column with square hollow section ☐ 400 × 10.0

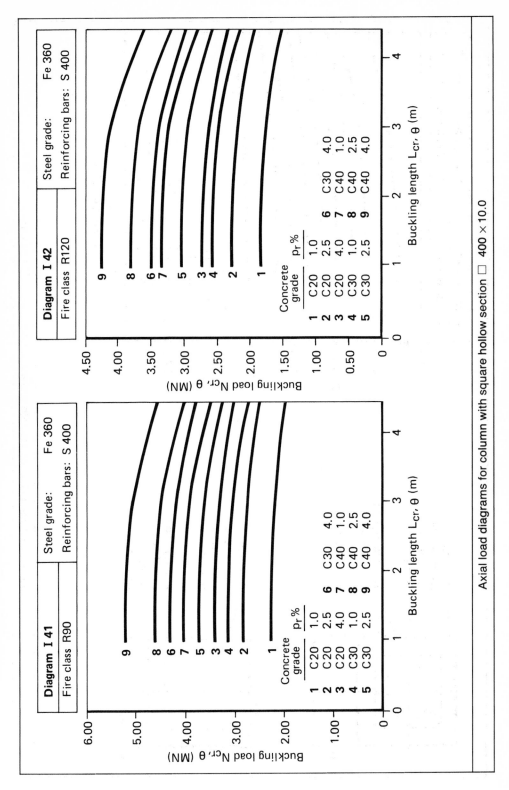

Axial load diagrams for column with square hollow section ☐ 400 × 10.0

Diagram I 41

Fire class R90

| Steel grade: | Fe 360 |
| Reinforcing bars: | S 400 |

	Concrete grade	p_r %			
1	C20	1.0	6	C30	4.0
2	C20	2.5	7	C40	1.0
3	C20	4.0	8	C40	2.5
4	C30	1.0	9	C40	4.0
5	C30	2.5			

Diagram I 42

Fire class R120

| Steel grade: | Fe 360 |
| Reinforcing bars: | S 400 |

	Concrete grade	p_r %			
1	C20	1.0	6	C30	4.0
2	C20	2.5	7	C40	1.0
3	C20	4.0	8	C40	2.5
4	C30	1.0	9	C40	4.0
5	C30	2.5			

Annex II:

Shear plate and shear design

II.1 Background: shear plate design

Recent experimental work [21] has quantified the performance of cleats. The design resistance (P_{RD}) can be expressed as:

$$P_{RD} = C_b \cdot f_{ck} \cdot A_c / \gamma_v$$

with C_b taken as the **lower** value of:

$$C_b = (1.0 + 35.0/f_{ck}) \sqrt{A_b/A_c}$$
$$C_b = 1.0$$

provided, $A_c/A_b < 25$

where, f_{ck} = characteristic concrete strength
$\quad\quad\ A_c$ = cross sectional area of concrete within the SHS
$\quad\quad\ A_b$ = bearing area of cleat
$\quad\quad\ \gamma_v$ = safety factor

The stated limits ensure that the cleat can neither be so thick that it could transmit a load in fire higher than the design compressive resistance of the concrete cross-section or be so thin that it crushes the concrete beneath it.

II.2 Background: shear stud design

Shear pins can be designed using Clause 6.3.2 of Eurocode 4, part 1 [16]. The design shear resistance (P_{RD}) will be the **lower** value of:

a) $\quad\quad P_{RD} = 0.29 \cdot \alpha \cdot d^2 \cdot \sqrt{f_{ck} \cdot E_{c,m}}/\gamma_v$ (based on local crushing of the concrete)

$\quad$ with, $\quad \alpha = 0.2 \cdot [1 + h/d]$ (for $h/d \leq 4$)
$\quad$ or, $\quad\ \alpha = 1.0$ $\quad\quad\quad\quad\quad$ (for $h/d > 4$)

or b) $\quad\quad P_{RD} = 0.8 \cdot f_u \cdot (\pi \cdot d^2/4)/\gamma_v$
$\quad\quad\quad\quad$ (based on stud shear strength)

$\quad$ where, $E_{c,m}$ = effective modulus of elasticity for the concrete
$\quad\quad\quad\ f_{ck}$ = characteristic concrete strength
$\quad\quad\quad\ f_u$ = ultimate tensile strength of stud
$\quad\quad\quad\ d$ = shear stud diameter
$\quad\quad\quad\ h$ = length of stud embedded in the concrete core
$\quad\quad\quad\ \gamma_v$ = safety factor

If the SHS outer shell of a column is left exposed in the area of the connection, it will lose most of its load carrying capacity in the event of a fire. Accordingly, the room temperature partial safety factor ($\gamma_v = 1.25$) should be used in both solutions in order to ensure that a connection will transmit its load safely in fire and the beam loads are fully transmitted into the concrete core.

II.3 Design example

Connectors are to be designed to transmit a balanced load from two beams at a fire design load of 175 kN/beam to a $260 \times 260 \times 6.3$ SHS-column filled with C 30 concrete.

There are two possible design solutions:

1. use a steel shear plate (see fig. 6.3)
2. use a steel seating bracket with shear studs (see fig. 6.4).

1) Shear plate design

Imposed fire design bearing load: $2 \cdot 175 = 350$ kN.

Assume that the shear plate is 12 mm thick, then:

Cross sectional area of concrete (A_c)
$$= (260 - 2 \cdot 6.3)^2 = 61,210 \text{ mm}^2$$

Bearing area of cleat (A_b)
$$= (260 - 2 \cdot 6.3) \cdot 12 = 29,690 \text{ mm}^2$$

$A_c/A_b = 612.1/29.69 = 20.61$ (< 25, so proportions OK)

$C_b \quad = (1 + 35.0/30.0) \cdot \sqrt{29.69/612.1} = 0.477$ (< 1, so OK)

so, $P_{RD} = 0.477 \cdot 30.0 \cdot 612.1 \cdot 10^{-1}/1.5 = \textbf{584 kN} > 350$ kN, so design OK

2) Shear stud design

If four shear studs are used for each seating bracket, then:

Imposed fire design shear load $= 175/4 = 43.75$ kN/stud

Assume studs are 16 mm dia. (d) $\times$ 100 mm long (h) and have a specified ultimate tensile strength (f_u) of 350 N/mm². According to Clause 6.3.2 of Eurocode 4, Part 1, the design shear resistance (P_{RD}) will be the **lower** value of:

a) $\quad P_{RD} = 0.29 \cdot \alpha \cdot d^2 \cdot \sqrt{f_{ck} \cdot E_{c,m}}/\gamma_v$

$\quad\quad h/d = 100/16 = 6.25 > 4$, so $\alpha = 1$

and $P_{RD} = 0.29 \cdot 1.0 \cdot 16^2 \cdot 10^{-3} \cdot \sqrt{30 \cdot 32,000}/1.25 = 58.19$ kN

b) $\quad P_{RD} = 0.8 \cdot f_u \cdot (\pi \cdot d^2/4)/\gamma_v$

$\quad\quad = 0.8 \cdot 350 \cdot 10^{-3} \cdot (\pi \cdot 16^2/4)/1.25$

$\quad\quad = \textbf{45.04 kN}$ (> 43.75 kN, so design OK)

Annex III:
A simple assessment of a water filled column structure

Assumptions:
A multi-storey building has been constructed using 200 sq SHS columns. Column spacings are as shown in Fig. III.1. The fire exposed length of each type of column is shown in Fig. III.2. The building has been zoned into individual one storey fire compartments each containing six columns (4 external/2 internal).

Requested:
What volume of water is needed in a zone to provide 60 minutes fire resistance? What will be the size of water tank needed (in m³) per zone? What will the water and steam flow rates be (in kg/min) in the pipework system after 60 minutes in fire?

It is assumed that the fire is restricted to one storey.

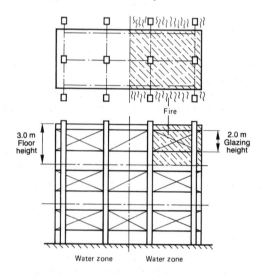

Fig. III.1 – Showing water zones and fire area

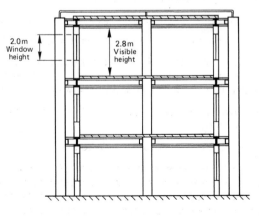

Fig. III.2

a) Volume of cooling water needed per zone

Assume that the external columns are close enough to the building to be fully immersed in flames at each window, with a window height of 2.0 m.

i. e. surface area of an external column exposed to fire

$= 4 \times 0.200 \times 2.00 = 1.60\ m^2$

From Table 5.2, water requirement for a 60 minute fire $= 82\ kg/m^2$

So, water required for an external column $= 82 \times 1.60 = 131.2\ kg/column$

Each internal column is to be fully exposed for a height of 2.8 m
So, exposed surface area of an internal column

$= 4 \times 0.200 \times 2.80 = 2.24\ m^2$

and water required for an internal column $= 82 \times 2.24 = 183.7\ kg/column$

So, total water required/zone $= 4 \times 131.2 + 2 \times 183.7 = 892.2\ kg \triangleq \mathbf{0.892\ m^3}$

b) Required Tank Volume per zone

Since this is a simple design, it is assumed that the steam is vented to the atmosphere through the free space in the water tank, that the tank is large enough to contain both the required cooling water + 10% extra (as a safety margin) and that it has sufficient additional volume to accept the water already contained by the columns in the fire zone (in the event that this water is temporarily expelled from the columns during an early period of unstable steam/water flow).

Approx. internal volume of a column $= 0.2 \times 0.2 \times 3.00 = 0.12\ m^3$

There are six columns per zone, so column volume/zone $= 6 \times 0.12 = 0.72\ m^3$

so, required tank volume $= 0.720 + 1.1 \times 0.892 = \mathbf{1.701\ m^3}$

i. e. a tank of dimensions 1 m high $\times$ 1.25 m wide $\times$ 1.5 long would be more than adequate.

c) Steam/water peak mass flow rates

Table III.1 (see below) gives the estimated peak water boil-off rate that would occur after continuous heating to the standard ISO fire curve for the stated fire times. Using this table, the steam generation rate and the necessary water replacement mass flow rate being produced within the system can now be estimated:

i. e. steam generation rate in an external column $= 2.0 \cdot 1.60 = 3.20\ kg/min/column$

and the steam generation rate in an internal column $= 2.0 \times 2.24 = 4.48\ kg/min/column$

These mass flow rates represent both the rate at which steam will leave a column to enter the steam vent pipeline system at the top of the column and also the rate at which replenishment water must enter a column from the water pipe work system.

So, the total water flow required within the down pipe from the header tank to replenish the whole fire zone is given by:

Total flow rate $= 4 \times 3.20 + 2 \times 4.48 = 21.76\ kg/min$

Figure III.3 shows the flow rates for the individual pipe lengths within the water/steam network for one zone. These flow rates must now be used in conjunction with standard steam and water friction coefficients, pressure head loss design formulae (or head loss design tables) and the pipe work geometry (i. e. steam and water pipe diameters, lengths, number of bends, etc.) to calculate the pressure head flow losses in the separate steam

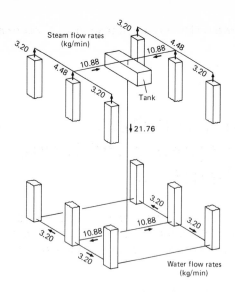

Fig. III.3 – Water and steam peak flow rates (kg/min) after 1 hour in fire

and water circuits. The pressure head needed to circulate the water and steam during any fire is then given by:

Total water head losses + total steam head losses.

This circulating pressure head is usually produced as a static head by ensuring that the base of the water tank is situated above the highest portion of column subject to flame impingement by that amount.

Note: If the tank has a top cover, then the steam will have to be vented from it. The additional pressure loss, this would generate, will also need to be included in the total head losses.

Table III.1: **Estimated peak water evaporation/steam production rates per m² heated column surface.**

Fire time (minutes)	30	60	90	120
Peak evaporation rate (kg/m²/min)	1.5	2.0	2.3	2.6
Equivalent peak steam production rates in m³/m²/sec at 1 bar	0.040	0.054	0.064	0.072

Comité International pour le Développement et l'Étude de la Construction Tubulaire

International Committee for the Development and Study of Tubular Structures

CIDECT founded in 1962 as an international association joins together the research resources of major hollow steel section manufacturers to create a major force in the research and application of hollow steel sections worldwide.

The objectives of CIDECT are:

○ to increase knowledge of hollow steel sections and their potential application by initiating and participating in appropriate researches and studies

○ to establish and maintain contacts and exchanges between the producers of the hollow steel sections and the ever increasing number of architects and engineers using hollow steel sections throughout the world.

○ to promote hollow steel section usage wherever this makes for good engineering practice and suitable architecture, in general by disseminating information, organizing congresses etc.

○ to co-operate with organizations concerned with practical design recommendations, regulations or standards at national and international level.

Technical activities

The technical activities of CIDECT have centred on the following research aspects of hollow steel section design:

○ Buckling behaviour of empty and concrete-filled columns
○ Effective buckling lengths of members in trusses
○ Fire resistance of concrete-filled columns
○ Static strength of welded and bolted joints
○ Fatigue resistance of joints
○ Aerodynamic properties
○ Bending strength
○ Corrosion resistance
○ Workshop fabrication

The results of CIDECT research form the basis of many national and international design requirements for hollow steel sections.

CIDECT, the future

Current work is chiefly aimed at filling up the gaps in the knowledge regarding the structural behaviour of hollow steel sections and the interpretation and implementation of the completed fundamental research. As this proceeds, a new complementary phase is opening that will be directly concerned with practical, economical and labour saving design.

CIDECT Publications

The current situation relating to CIDECT publications reflects the ever increasing emphasis on the dissemination of research results.

Apart from the final reports of the CIDECT sponsored research programmes, which are available at the Technical Secretariat on demand at nominal price, CIDECT has published a number of monographs concerning various aspects of design with hollow steel sections. These are available in English, French and German as indicated.

Monograph No. 3 – Windloads for Lattice Structures (G)
Monograph No. 4 – Effective Lengths of Lattice Girder Members (E, F, G)
Monograph No. 5 – Concrete-filled Hollow Section Columns (F)
Monograph No. 6 – The Strength and Behaviour of Statically Loaded Welded Connections in Structural Hollow Sections (E)
Monograph No. 7 – Fatigue Behaviour of Hollow Section Joints (E, G)

A book "Construction with Hollow Steel Sections", prepared under the direction of CIDECT in English, French, German and Spanish, was published with the sponsorship of the European Community presenting the actual state of the knowledge acquired throughout the world with regard to hollow steel sections and the design methods and application technologies related to them.

In addition, copies of these publications can be obtained from the individual members given below to whom technical questions relating to CIDECT work or the design using hollow steel sections should be addressed.

The organization of CIDECT comprises:

○ President: Dr. D. Russell (Federal Republic of Germany)
Vice-President: C. L. Bijl (The Netherlands)

○ A General Assembly of all members meeting once a year and appointing an Executive Committee responsible for adiministration and executing of estabished policy

○ Technical Commission and Working Groups meeting at least once a year and directly responsible for the research and technical promotion work

○ Secretariat in Mülheim responsible for the day to day running of the organization.

Present members of CIDECT are:

(1993)

○ British Steel PLC, United Kingdom
○ Hoogovens Buizen, The Netherlands
○ ILVA Form, Italy
○ IPSCO Inc., Canada
○ Laminaciones de Lesaca S.A., Spain
○ Laminoirs de Longtain, Belgium
○ Mannesmannröhren-Werke AG, Federal Republic of Germany
○ Mannstädt Werke GmbH, Federal Republic of Germany
○ Nippon Steel Metal Products Co. Ltd., Japan
○ Rautaruukki Oy, Finland
○ Sonnichsen A/S, Norway
○ Tubemakers of Australia, Australia
○ Van Leeuwen, The Nietherlands
○ Valexy, France
○ VOEST Alpine Krems, Austria

Cidect Research Reports can be obtained through:

Mr. D. Dutta
Office of the Chairman of the CIDECT Technical Commission
c/o Mannesmannröhren-Werke AG
Wiesenstrasse 36
45473 Mülheim an der Ruhr
Federal Republic of Germany

Telephone: (49) 208/458 1581
Telefax: (49) 208/458 1580